# FLINT BLADES
## and
# PROJECTILE POINTS
## of the North American Indian

by
Lawrence N. Tully

Photography
by
Steven N. Tully

**COLLECTOR BOOKS**
*A Division of Schroeder Publishing Co., Inc.*

Additional copies of this book may be ordered from:

Collector Books
P.O. Box 3009
Paducah, KY 42001

or

Lawrence N. Tully
Rt 7, Box 169
Benton, KY 42025

@ $24.95. Add $1.00 for postage and handling.

**TO THE MEMORY OF MY FATHER**

And the carefree days of my youth spent hunting arrowheads with

my friends along the Harris Fork and Bayou de Chien creeks


AND


**TO BARBARA**

Without whose support and encouragement this book could not
have been written

# ACKNOWLEDGEMENTS

I am grateful for the help of many people in writing this book. I am especially indebted to Ann Curtiss for granting me access to the Curtiss family collection, assembled by the late Eugene Curtiss, Sr., with its outstanding representation of southeastern Indian artifacts.

A special thanks must go to the Thomas Gilcrease Institute of American History and Art, Tulsa, Oklahoma, and its staff who, with enormous patience, assisted me and made available many pieces of outstanding flint from "old time" collections. This flint was acquired by the late Thomas Gilcrease and is now a permanent part of the Institute.

Special recognition must go to Quintis Herron, President of the Board of Directors of the Herron Research Foundation, and to the Museum of the Red River, Idabel, Oklahoma, which is supported by this foundation.

I am indebted to Gregory Perino for use of materials from his private collection, and for flint artifacts that he made available as director of the Museum of the Red River. Over the years, his information and advice has been most valuable to me.

Mary Thompson generously granted me access to the Russ Thompson family collection with its outstanding Fort Ancient types and other fine flint artifacts. The late Russ Thompson was greatly respected and appreciated by Indian artifact collectors for his work with the Green River Archaeological Society of Kentucky and other amateur groups.

Robert Edler, with whom I corresponded over the years, has never failed to give a careful and thorough answer to my many questions. It was through his help that I was able to identify several flint forms that are very important to this book.

A special thanks to Jack Roberts, Frank Morast, Jr., and Clement Caldwell, along with their wives, for the gracious southern hospitality extended to me and my family during photographic sessions in their homes, and at other times. Considerable time and effort was spent by them in removing flint artifacts from permanent mounts and storage.

A special thanks to Deborah Tully for technical advice and assistance on the format.

During the 12 years that this book was researched and written, I was privileged to meet and cultivate the friendship of numerous other collectors of North American Indian artifacts. Of these collectors, many contributed to this book by furnishing outstanding flint artifacts from their private collections or provided valuable publications for research purposes. Several people contributed information about locations of fine flint examples, were helpful in discussing archaeological data about point types, and most important of all, extended interest and encouragement.

I wish to apologize if any contributor was inadvertently omitted from the following list:

Ralph Allen, Jr., Montgomery, Alabama
Son Anderson, Cusseta, Alabama
Dale Van Blair, Belleville, Illinois
Dr. Neal Brown, Columbus, Georgia
Mark Clark, Clarksville, Tennessee
Robert Crosier, Mauckport, Indiana
Howard Cross, Savannah, Tennessee
Gene Curtiss, Jr., Benton, Kentucky
John DeLime, Murray, Kentucky
Pat Fleming, Alton, Illinois
Kenneth Ford, Benton, Kentucky
Leland Hasler, Newberry, Indiana
Tom Hendrix, Florence, Alabama
Robin Hornsby, Holly Hill, Florida
Randal Jones, Paoli, Indiana
Ray Kilgore, Cusseta, Alabama
Ronald Knight, Chattanooga, Tennessee
Donald Leutjen, Cole Camp, Missouri
Bob Lindley, Paoli, Indiana
David Lutz, Newburgh, Indiana
Leonard Moore, Litchfield, Kentucky
Willie Palmer, Mt. Eden, Kentucky

Irwin Peek, Jasper, Alabama
Dorothy Perino, Idabel, Oklahoma
Kevin Pipes, Pigeon Forge, Tennessee
Doug Puckett, Sheffield, Alabama
Dennis Quintavalle, Decatur, Alabama
Robert Rea, Decatur, Alabama
Jan Riley, Holly Hill, Florida
Floyd Ritter, Collinsville, Illinois
Don Sailer, Paoli, Indiana
H. B. Sisemore, Salina, Oklahoma
David Smith, Savannah, Tennessee
Frank Standhart, Miller, Missouri
Dale Strader, Calvert City, Kentucky
Ben Thompson, St. Louis, Missouri
Tim Thompson, Versailles, Kentucky
John Tilley, Chattanooga, Tennessee
Tommy Tucker, Tunica, Mississippi
Mark Waggener, III, Germantown, Tennessee
Becky Wilkes, Savannah, Tennessee
Jeff Wilkes, Savannah, Tennessee
Jimmy Wilkes, Savannah, Tennessee
Gary Williams, Florence, Alabama

# TABLE OF CONTENTS

# INDEX OF TYPES

# INTRODUCTION

This book is written for students and collectors of North American Indian artifacts. It is the result of many hours of research and correspondence, endless miles of travel, and the efforts and cooperation of numerous Indian artifact collectors.

Many outstanding collector museums and private collections aren't accessible or well-known. Flint artifacts from some of these collector museums and private collections, as well as several outstanding flint artifacts that were owned by well-known "old time" collectors, are presented for the first time in this publication. References are made where other flint artifacts appear in publications known to the author, or are thought to be appropriate to the text.

Some flint blades and projectile point forms, referred to in this book, have been named and dated in literature by archaeologists, or others, using locations where they were presumably first recognized. Names of flint blades and projectile points are used in the text for general reference only. The reader should understand that examples shown in any given case may or may not be the type suggested by the accompanying reference name. The Selected Reference section in the back of this book should be consulted for particular information.

All of the artifacts shown in this book are as near actual size as is practicable. Slight variations in scale are due to technical variables inherent in the photographic process.

The numbers represent the sequence in which the items were photographed by Steven Tully.

**701**
**Humphreys Co., Tenn.**

   This flint face is one of four bearing the J. T. Reeder collection Nos. 271, 272, 273 and 274 and were found in a stone box burial near Waverly, Tennessee, by M. Hobbs in 1902. Two of these flint faces bearing the Nos. 271 and 274 are in the Thomas Gilcrease Institute of American History and Art in Tulsa, Oklahoma. The face shown here bearing the No. 273 is in the Jack C. Roberts collection in Tunica, Mississippi. The location of No. 272 is unknown to the author. For additional information see Roberts (1968).

   These faces are unique in North American archaeology. No other examples are known.

332

**Reference:** See Kerrville Knives and Old World hand axes.

**Comments:** The blades shown here are from Kerr County, Texas. For further information on this type of blade in North America, see Macgowan and Hester (1962).

333

875
Ballard Co., Ky.

876
(Western Kentucky)

**Reference:** See beveled knives and preforms.

**Comments:** Typical examples of this form with the base down have the beveling on the left hand side of each face. This method of resharpening results in a rhomboid cross-section, a feature that is also found on resharpened projectile points such as the "deep-notch," "dove-tail," Meserve, Breckenridge, Greenbrier, and others. In some forms the bevel may occur on the right hand side of the blade but this is extremely rare in the "deep-notch" and "dove-tail" forms.

874
Lawrence Co., Tenn.

669
Lyon Co., Ky.

**Reference:** No data.

**Comments:** This class of blade, as with the Ohio River Valley forms, appears to have a special significance other than utilitarian use.

10

**673**
**Hardin Co., Ky.**

**Reference:** No data.

**Comments:** Large blades, such as the form shown here, are seldom modified by notching and resharpening. Specimens of this quality and size are believed to have a special significance other than utilitarian use. Rounded base forms are found throughout the Ohio River Valley and are often made from colorful Ohio Flint Ridge material.

824
Bullitt Co., Ky.

668
Ohio

**Reference:** No data.

**Comments:** The examples shown here belong to the same pattern as No. 673. The transverse parallel flaking shown on No. 824 is an unusual treatment of this type. No. 668 is made of Ohio Flint Ridge chalcedony. See the Diller Spear for the notched form (Thompson, 1968:120).

**675**
**Benton Co., Tenn.**

**680**
**Henry Co., Tenn.**

**679**
**Henry Co., Tenn.**

**Reference:** No data.

**Comments:** These examples are similar to forms found in shell mound context along the Tennessee River (Webb and DeJarnette, 1942). To the author's knowledge, the form has not been named in the southeastern United States. The material is Dover, Tennessee, flint.

13

**Reference:** See Wadlow.

**Comments:** For information on the Wadlow form see Perino (1968a). The example shown here is typical of the Wadlow form. Lengths may exceed 12 inches in some cases. Material is usually white or gray flint.

**131**
**Missouri (Co. unknown)**

311
Oklahoma

312
St. Louis Co., Mo.

**Reference:** See beveled ovoid blades.

**Comments:** When new this blade form is oval and may have from one to four beveled edges. Similar forms from Texas have four beveled edges and are called Harahey Knives. The Harahey Knife form is believed to have been reproduced in recent years.

15

| 670 | 672 | 674 |
| :---: | :---: | :---: |
| Lowndes Co., Miss. | Warrick Co., Ind. | Perry Co., Tenn. |

**Reference:** See bi-pointed knives and preforms.

**Comments:** Three bi-pointed forms are shown here for comparison. No. 672 appears to be a transitional form. The rounded end indicates a more specialized use such as a hand-held knife, preform for a stemmed based blade, or projectile point. Blades similar to Nos. 670 and 674 are often mistaken for the Lerma form, an early southwestern projectile point.

16

683       684       682       681

**Reference:** The examples shown here are pictured by LaDassor (1966a). See bi-pointed knives.

**Comments:** Nos. 683 and 684 are from a cache of 44 blades found near Clinton in Hickman County, Kentucky, in June, 1965. No. 683 of this cache is pictured on page 55 in the lower right hand corner of the plate and No. 684 is shown on page 54 on the left hand side of the plate in the above cited reference. Nos. 681 and 682 are pictured in the plate shown on page 53 also in the above cited reference and are from a cache of 37 blades found near Almo in Calloway County, Kentucky. The two caches were found approximately 50 miles apart and 30 miles from the source of material. The blades in both caches are made from Dover, Tennessee, flint.

752

751

**Reference:** No. 751 is pictured by Van Blair (1983b). See Adena blades (southeastern form).

**Comments:** For a comparison between the Ohio Adena and the Tennessee Adena, see Lewis and Kneberg (1957b). The two blades shown here are from a group of 14 blades found near Clifton in Wayne County, Tennessee, on the north bank of the Tennessee River in the Spring of 1977. Nine of these blades were found in a definite cache. The material is white flint with a pink cast and is characteristic of other examples found in the Pickwick Basin area. For other examples of this form see Duncan (1973a).

694

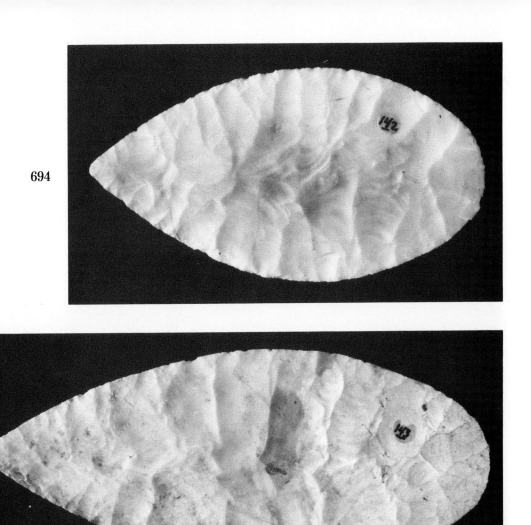

693

692

**Reference:** See Adena blades (southeastern form).

**Comments:** This cache of three blades was found in Colbert County, Alabama, in 1939 by E. E. Curtiss, Sr. The material is the same as Nos. 751 and 752.

**229**
**Montgomery Co., Mo.**

**Reference:** See North Blades and North Points.

**Comments:** This blade form is the preform for the Illinois Hopewell Snyders and is often made of colorful Illinois heat-treated flint. For further information on the North form, see Perino (1971a).

230

346

347

**Reference:** Nos. 346 and 351 are pictured by Perino (1969b). See North Points or North Blades.

**Comments:** These three examples are part of a cache of 53 blades found in North Mound 2 in Clinton County, Illinois.

351

**551**
**Columbia Co., Ark.**

**144**
**Wabash Co., Ill.**

**268**
**Marinette Co., Wisc.**

**Reference:** Nos. 268 and 144 are pictured by Grimm (1953:35). See Clovis and Enterline forms.

**Comments:** This fluted form is typically large in size and is often wide in proportion to length. It is characterized by the use of large flakes in its construction and has a minimum of retouch along the edges. This is an extremely rare form and few examples have been reported in North America. To the author's knowledge, this form has not been reported in archaeological context.

**407**
**Cumberland Co., Ky.**

**36**

**39**
**Arkansas**

**Reference:** See Clovis and Enterline forms.

**Comments:** The examples shown here are contracting base forms and belong to the same pattern as Nos. 144, 268, and 551.

**559**
**Cherokee Co., N.C.**

**558**
**Barren Co., Ky.**

**916**
**Hines Co., Miss.**

**Reference:** See Clovis, Enterline, and Folsom forms.

**Comments:** Three fluted forms are shown here for comparison. Note the multiple flake thinning of the base on No. 559 and the remnant of the fluting platform with the negative bulb of percussion on No. 558. No. 916 is similar to the Folsom form but the fluting and flaking is inferior to the Folsom.

**Reference:** This example is pictured by Young (1910) and by Grimm (1953:57). See Clovis and Enterline forms.

**Comments:** The fluting on this form does not appear to be as advanced technically as the Folsom or Cumberland forms. Usually in the thinning of the base, one large flake was removed from one or both sides. Often these large flakes are not in the center of the base and tend to veer off at an angle to the longitudinal axis of the blade. Additional flakes were usually taken off to complete the thinning. This basal thinning procedure is similar to the Enterline technique.

785
Warren Co., Ky.

**243**
**Madison Co., Ky.**

**37**
**Warrick Co., Ind.**

**815**
**Edmonson Co., Ky.**

**Reference:** See Clovis and Enterline forms.

**Comments:** The examples shown here represent two distinct forms of the fluted point. The large contracting base forms similar to No. 243 appear to be somewhat earlier than the narrow straight-sided forms Nos. 37 and 815. These narrow straight-sided forms are called Clovis. To the author's knowledge, the large contracting base form has not been named.

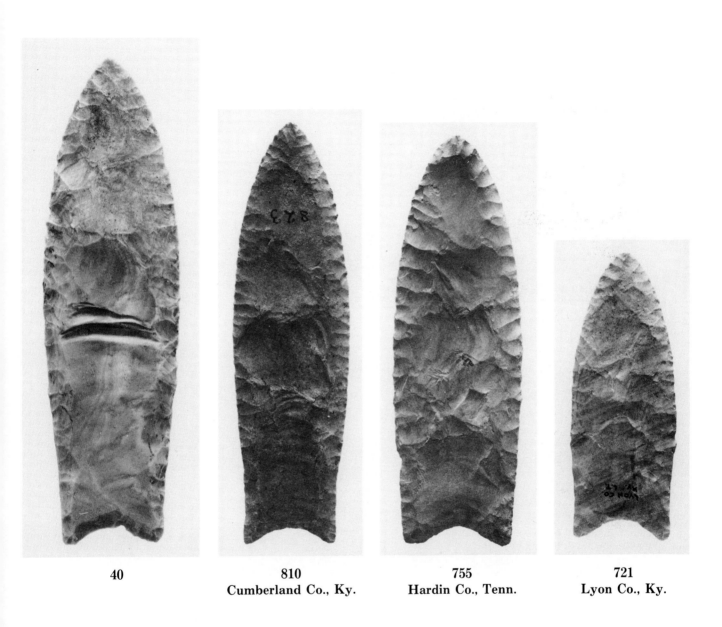

| 40 | 810<br>Cumberland Co., Ky. | 755<br>Hardin Co., Tenn. | 721<br>Lyon Co., Ky. |

**Reference:** See Clovis, Enterline, and Ross County (fluted).

**Comments:** The fluted form shown here has a slight beveling of the edges on both faces of the blade. This beveling produces a flat-hexagonal cross-section. It is not clear if this beveling is a result of resharpening or if the blade was constructed this way initially. The fluting is typically shallow and in many cases the fluting flake does not hinge out. For information on this form see Perino (1971a).

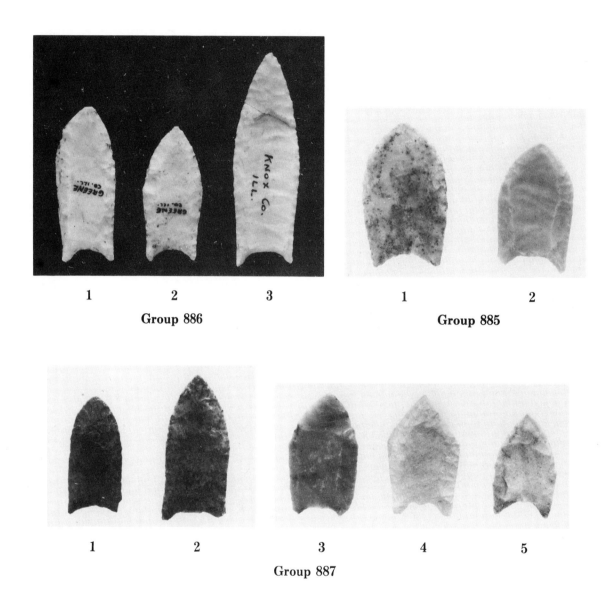

1       2       3

**Group 886**

1       2

**Group 885**

1       2       3       4       5

**Group 887**

**Reference:** See Folsom.

**Comments:** In Group 885 No. 1 is from western New Mexico and No. 2 is from El Paso County, Texas. In Group 886 Nos. 1 and 2 are from Greene County, Illinois and No. 3 is from Knox County, Illinois. In Group 887, all examples are from El Paso County, Texas. The Group 886 examples are tentatively identified as Folsom forms.

28

**Reference:** See Conerly.

**Comments:** For information on the Conerly point, see Cambron and Hulse (1975).

**687**
**Lawrence Co., Tenn.**

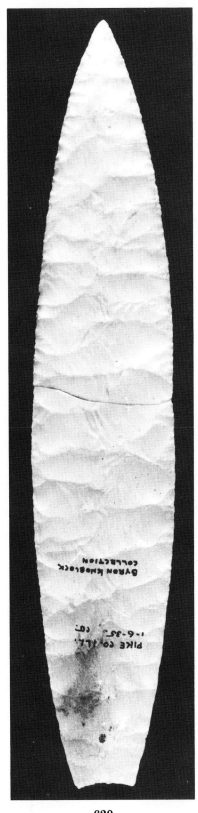

**Reference:** See Agate Basin, Sedalia, Nebo Hill, and others.

**Comments:** For information on this form, see Perino (1968a).

630
Pike Co., Ill.

**30**
Saline Co., Mo.

**27**
Pike Co., Ill.

**108**
Pike Co., Ark.

**343**
Bastrop Co., Tx.

**Reference:** See No. 630.

**Comments:** For information on the Agate Basin form, see Wormington (1958). No. 343 has been designated Texas Agate Basin by Perino. For information on the Mahaffey Point No. 108, see Perino (1977).

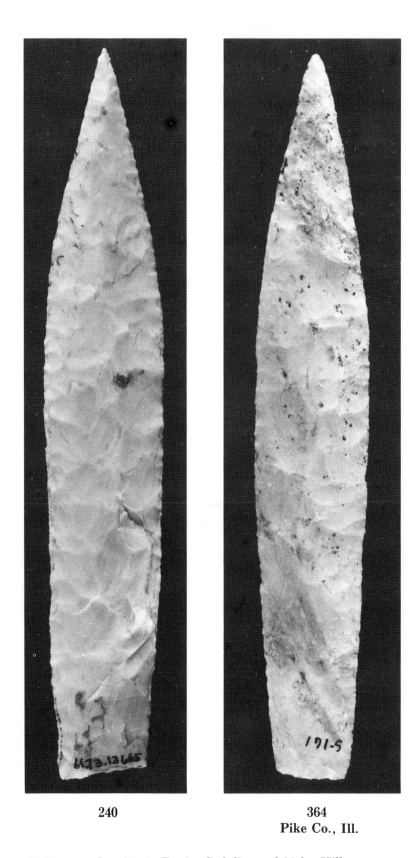

240

364
Pike Co., Ill.

**Reference:** See Agate Basin, Sedalia, and Nebo Hill.

**Comments:** The examples shown here are representative of the Sedalia form and compare in workmanship with the Nebo Hill rather than the Agate Basin. The typical Agate Basin is superior in workmanship to the other two forms. Well executed examples of the Sedalia form are often confused with the Agate Basin.

**7**
Pettis Co., Mo.

**8**
Pettis Co., Mo.

**9**
Henry Co., Mo.

**Reference:** See Agate Basin, Hell Gap, and others.

**Comments:** Perino (1984) states that this point has a rare occurrence and is possibly related to the Agate Basin-Hell Gap forms. The form has not been named in Missouri.

279                    275                    277

**Reference:** Nos. 275 and 279 are pictured by Grimm (1953:111). No. 275 is pictured by Perino (1968a). See Red Ochre points.

**Comments:** Perino states that "turkey-tail" forms are found associated with this form. The three blades shown here are from a cache of 50 from St. Clair County, Illinois, cited in the above reference.

**289**
**Greene Co., Ill.**

**Obverse and Reverse
sides shown**

**Reference:** This blade is pictured by Perino (1963, 1971b). See Ramey Knife.

**Comments:** Perino states that the Ramey Knife is most often made from Mill Creek (Union County, Illinois) flint. Other examples are made from Kaolin (Illinois novaculite), or native white flint. The reverse side of the blade is encrusted with red ochre stained calcite.

676
Hamilton Co., Tenn.
(Williams Island)

Obverse              Reverse

292
Greene Co., Ill.

**Reference:** No. 292 is pictured by Perino (1963, 1971b). See Ramey Knife and others.

**Comments:** See No. 289 for information on the Ramey Knife. To the author's knowledge, this blade form has not been named in Tennessee or Kentucky.

878                                    879                                    880

**Reference:** No data.

**Comments:** The three blades shown here are from a cache of eight blades found in Hickman County, Kentucky. Of the eight blades in the cache, all but one appear to have been made from resolved flakes, a flaking technique characteristic of the Paleo-Indian complex. The bulbar end of the flake in this case being used for the "handle" end. For information on flake types see Lewis and Kneberg (1962). To the author's knowledge, this form has not been named in Kentucky.

**305**
**Sheboygan Co., Wisc.**

**Reference:** See Morse Archaic Knife.

**Comments:** This knife form is similar to No. 11 shown by Grimm (1953:65). For information on the Morse Archaic Knife form see Perino (1969a). These knife forms are sometimes referred to as "handled daggers" or "flint daggers".

304
Monroe Co., Ill.

287
Boone Co., Mo.

306
St. Louis Co., Mo.

**Reference:** See Morse Archaic Knife.

**Comments:** These examples show some of the variations of this knife form.

**214**
**Howard Co., Ark.**
**(Manning Jones Place)**

**Reference:** See Mineral Springs knife.

**Comments:** The Mineral Springs and Gahagan knife forms are related but the form shown here is somewhat older (Perino, 1984).

**664**
**Jefferson Co., Ark.**

**318**

**322**

**Reference:** Nos. 318 and 322 are pictured by Perino (1976b). See Mineral Springs and Gahagan knives.

**Comments:** The Mineral Springs and Gahagan knife forms are shown here for comparison. Typical blade edges of both forms are recurved but the Mineral Springs has an incurved basal edge. Nos. 318 and 322 are typical Gahagan knives. No. 664 is the classic Mineral Springs.

321                                329                                323

**Reference:** Nos. 321, 323, and 326 are pictured by Burford (1948) and by Perino (1976b). See Kinney points.

**Comments:** For information on the Kinney form, see Bell (1958).

326

356         358         357

**Reference:** See Refugio points.

**Comments:** For information on the Refugio form, see Bell (1968).

328                    324                    327

**Reference:** Nos. 324 and 328 are pictured by Perino (1976b). See Pandora points.

**Comments:** For information on the Pandora points, see Bell (1960).

932                    13                    14

**Reference:** No. 932 is pictured by Scott (1974). See Copena.

**Comments:** No. 932 is one of a cache of 50 blades found in Hardin County, Tennessee, in 1970. Nos. 13 and 14 are from a cache of four blades found near Cravens Landing in Hardin County, Tennessee. There appears to be two distinctly different forms of Copena. No. 932 shown here is the straight sided form and Nos. 13 and 14 are the "shield" form. Both forms are shown by Webb and DeJarnette (1942, Plate 29). The "shield" shape is typical of the form.

**Group 205**
**Yell County, Arkansas**
**(Cardon Bottom)**

**Reference:** See Nodena and ''willow-leaf'' forms.

**Comments:** For information on the Nodena form, see Bell (1958).

**Group 374**
**Mason Co., Ky.**


**Reference:** See Fort Ancient.

**Comments:** The serrated examples shown in the above group have been named Fort Ancient from the Fort Ancient site in southwestern Ohio. The non-serrated forms shown in the above group, also found on Fort Ancient sites, are similar to the Hamilton and Madison forms. This form of serrated point is identified with the Fort Ancient Culture.

47

**Group 338**
**Red River County, Texas**

**Reference:** See Maud and Hamilton points.

**Comments:** For information on the Maud point, see Bell (1958).

**Group 119**
**Cocke Co., Tenn.**

**Reference:** See Camp Creek and Del Rio points.

**Comments:** The form shown above was predominant at the multiple burial site at Del Rio near Newport in Cocke County, Tennessee. Similar forms found at the Camp Creek site in Greene County, Tennessee, have been named Camp Creek by Lewis and Kneberg (1957a). The examples shown here are made from red jasper.

368
Barren Co., Ky.

830
Montgomery Co., Tenn.

834
Tishomingo Co., Miss.

**Reference:** See Frazier and others.

**Comments:** For information on the Frazier form, see Kneberg (1956).

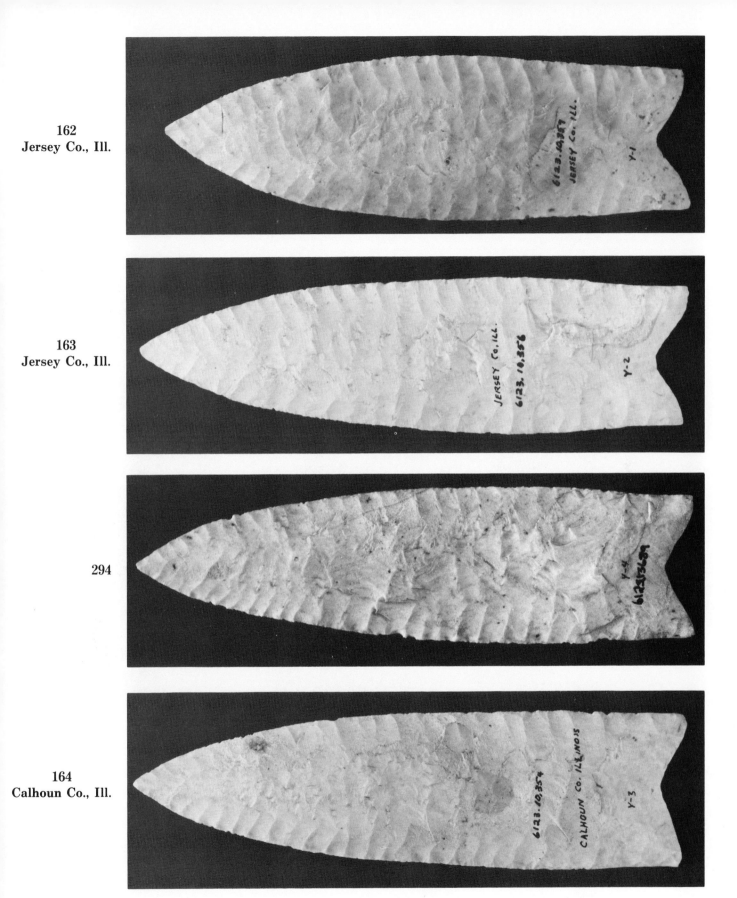

**162**
**Jersey Co., Ill.**

**163**
**Jersey Co., Ill.**

**294**

**164**
**Calhoun Co., Ill.**

**Reference:** Nos. 162, 163, and 164 are pictured by Fowler (1951:16). See Dalton.

**Comments:** Examples of the size and workmanship shown here are extremely rare. This form is frequently referred to as a "first-stage" Dalton. Some of the Dalton forms are believed to have been reproduced in recent years.

34
St. Louis Co., Mo.

28

29

**Reference:** No. 34 is pictured by Grimm (1953:97). See Dalton and others.

**Comments:** These three examples are shown here for comparison. Nos. 28 and 29 are resharpened forms. No. 29 is resharpened by beveling on the left side on both faces of the blade. No. 34 represents the initial shape of this form.

543
Pike Co., Ill.

690
Pike Co., Ill.

542
Marion Co., Mo.

**Reference:** See Pike form.

**Comments:** This form has been named by Perino (1982) for examples found in Pike County, Illinois, and the adjacent area in Missouri. An example of the form No. 690 is shown by Duncan (1972). There is some variation in the base but No. 542 is probably the typical form.

330
Cherokee Co., Okla.

804
St. Francis Co., Ark.

245
Cross Co., Ark.

**Reference:** No. 245 is pictured by Perino (1967a). See Dalton and others.

**Comments:** No. 330 represents one of the finest examples of this eared form on record from Oklahoma (Perino, 1983). The basal notch is deeper and the ears more pronounced on this form than on the classic Dalton. For an almost identical example of No. 330 from Illinois, see Duncan (1972).

**801**
**St. Louis Co., Mo.**

**541**
**Missouri**

**649**
**Pike Co., Mo.**

**802**
**Madison Co., Ill.**

**648**
**Pike Co., Ill.**

**Reference:** See Dalton and others.

**Comments:** Typical examples of this form are not beveled when resharpened. It is difficult to recognize the Dalton type before resharpening. Nos. 801 and 864 are probably near the classic form. Examples similar to No. 864 were found at the Bull Brook site near Ipswich, Massachusetts (Wormington, 1958). The fluting on the Bull Brook examples appears to be more definite than on the Dalton form. For information on the Dalton, see Bell (1958).

**650**
**Missouri**

**864**
**Pike Co., Ill.**

**568, Davidson Co., Tenn.**

**567, Marshall Co., Ky.**

**812, Hardin Co., Ky.**

**409, Breckinridge Co., Ky.**

**300, Licking Co., Ohio**

**38, Tennessee River**

**Reference:** See Cumberland and "Ohio fluted."

**Comments:** The single flute flaking technique is highly developed in the Cumberland form and is comparable and often superior to that of the Folsom. Remnants of the fluting platform occurs in this form suggesting the same fluting technique as in the Clovis, Enterline, and Folsom forms. The area of distribution is primarily in the southeastern United States. Examples are found along the Cumberland and Tennessee Rivers but the form is extremely rare everywhere. Converse (1973) states that this form is probably the rarest of all fluted points in Ohio.

125, Perry County, Tenn.

**Reference:** See Greenbrier (Dalton) and Breckenridge (Dalton).

**Comments:** For information on the two forms, see Bell (1960) and Perino (1971a).

384, Hardin County, Tenn.

435, Hardin County, Tenn.

53, Hardin County, Tenn.

466, Lyon County, Ky.

**385**
**Hardin Co., Tenn.**

**532**
**Tennessee**

**534**
**Tennessee**

**535**
**Benton Co., Tenn.**

**Reference:** See Rowan points.

**Comments:** Cooper (1970) states that Rowan points are believed to be the transitional form of the Dalton-Meserve, Quad, and Hardaway forms to Archaic corner-notched and side-notched forms. In the lower Tennessee River Valley, the Rowan form may be confused with the Greenbrier with more distinct side notches.

250      251      252      257

253      256      254      255

**Reference:** See Rowan points and others.

**Comments:** The examples shown here are from southwest Arkansas. The form has not been named in Arkansas but Perino (1985a) states that they are believed to be an unnamed variety of Dalton. The material is novaculite.

| 84 | 86 | 83 |
|:---:|:---:|:---:|
| Pasco Co., Fla. | Hillsborough Co., Fla. | Hillsborough Co., Fla. |

**Reference:** No. 84 is pictured by Van Blair (1982a). See Suwannee and Simpson.

**Comments:** The Suwannee and Simpson forms are shown here for comparison. The example of the Suwannee No. 84 is one of the finest recorded from Florida. For information on the two forms, see Bullen (1958).

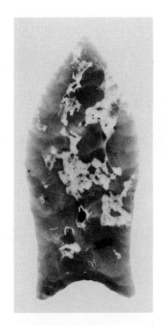

**83**
**Hillsborough Co., Fla.**

**235**
**Pike Co., Ark.**

**918**
**Tate Co., Miss.**

**Reference:** See Coldwater, Simpson, Pelican, Beaver Lake, and Quad.

**Comments:** For a discussion of the relationship between the Coldwater No. 918, Pelican No. 235, Simpson No. 83, Quad and Beaver Lake forms, see McGahey (1981).

**560**
**Lawrence Co., Tenn.**

**561**
**Tennessee**

**563**
**Lyon Co., Ky.**

**562**
**Lyon Co., Ky.**

**564**
**Tennessee**

**Reference:** See Beaver Lake.

**Comments:** Nos. 561 and 564 represent the classic form. The examples shown here illustrate the variations within the form. This pattern may be confused with the Greenbrier (Dalton) and the Quad. It has been called "unfluted Cumberland" by other writers (Perino, 1968a).

369
Bourbon Co., Ky.

658

768
Montgomery Co., Tenn.

**Reference:** See Quad.

**Comments:** The examples shown here are probably the shape of the Quad form before resharpening. This form was resharpened by the flat flaking technique and it is often difficult to determine the initial shape and length. For information on the Quad form, see Cambron and Hulse (1975). Examples of the size shown here are rare.

553
Crittenden Co., Ky.

552
Hardin Co., Tenn.

554

557

556

555

**Reference:** See Quad.

**Comments:** Nos. 554 and 556 represent the classic form. Nos. 554, 555, 556, and 557 are from Hart County, Kentucky. For information on the Quad form, see Bell (1960).

575

900
Texas

370
Posey Co., Ind.

540

576

539

**Reference:** No. 370 is pictured by LaDassor (1958a) and by Duncan (1973b:182). See Golondrina.

**Comments:** For information on the Golondrina, see Perino (1971a). Nos. 539, 540, 575, and 576 are from Graves County, Kentucky.

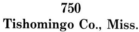

| 750 | 833 | 762 |
|-----|-----|-----|
| Tishomingo Co., Miss. | Tishomingo Co., Miss. | Limestone Co., Ala. |

**Reference:** No. 762 is pictured by Lewis and Kneberg (1953), Bell (1960), and Puckett (1983). See Wheeler and others.

**Comments:** The distributional area for this form is roughly from North Carolina westward through Alabama. The typical shape represented by Nos. 750 and 762 has a flat-hexagonal cross-section, slight incurvature at the sides of the base, and a square-like incurvature of the basal edge that is steeply beveled on both faces of the blade. Some triangular forms found in the area of distribution may be confused with this form. The form is extremely rare with few examples known.

544   846   545   33   854

853   848   502   546

**Reference:** Eared forms.

**Comments:** The examples shown here are various eared forms from western Kentucky, Tennessee, and surrounding areas. No. 33 is a rare form from the Tennessee River area and was originally named Eva by Lewis and Kneberg (1951). Nos. 544, 545, 502, and 546 are beveled on the left side of the blade. No. 502 is identical to the Dalton form No. 29 in this publication.

436
Hart Co., Ky.

571
Tennessee

572
Tennessee

573
Benton Co., Tenn.

**Reference:** No data.

**Comments:** The author has encountered one other example identical to No. 436 from Ohio County, Kentucky. The others shown here may be variations of the Greenbrier (Dalton) but the workmanship is inferior to the typical Greenbrier. To the author's knowledge, the form represented by No. 436 has not been named.

1                              2

**Group 912**
**Hinds Co., Miss.**

910                            913
**Hinds Co., Miss.**          **Simpson Co., Miss.**

**Reference:** See Hinds Point.

**Comments:** For information on the Hinds form, see McGahey (1981).

1
Simpson Co., Miss.

2
Tishomingo Co., Miss.

Group 911

1

2

Group 915
Hinds Co., Miss.

1
Simpson Co., Miss.

2
Rankin Co., Miss.

Group 914

**Reference:** See Dalton variety Hester, Hardaway, and San Patrice.

**Comments:** The form shown here has been named Dalton variety Hester from the Hester Site in Monroe County, Mississippi. The archaeological work at the Hester Site is part of an on-going project by Sam Brooks of the Mississippi Department of Archives and History (McGahey, 1985). For examples of the Hardaway form from the St. Albans and Doerschuk-Hardaway sites, see Broyles (1971:45). For examples of the San Patrice form, see Bell (1958).

**233**
**Colorado**

**891**
**Southeast Colorado**

**211**
**Colorado**

**889**
**West New Mexico**

**Reference:** No. 211 is pictured by Perino (1968a, 1971a).
See Rio Grande and Hell Gap points.

**Comments:** The Hell Gap form, Nos. 233 and 891, and
the Rio Grande form, Nos. 211 and 889, are shown here
for comparison.

905          909          906

907          908          904

**Reference:** No data.

**Comments:** The examples shown here are similar to the Sumter form shown by Bullen (1968), the Rio Grande form shown by Perino (1968a) and the Durst form found in Wisconsin. The points shown here are from Warren County, Kentucky. To the author's knowledge, this form has not been named in Kentucky.

319                  453                  527
           Benton Co., Tenn.

**Reference:** See Adena.

**Comments:** The three examples shown here are representative of the Adena forms described by Converse (1973). The Cresap form No. 319 and the Robbins form No. 527 are from Ohio. The total distributional area for the Adena form is not known. No. 453 from Tennessee is very much like the Early and Middle Adena forms. For information on the Tennessee Adena, see Lewis and Kneberg (1957b). No. 527 is made from Knife River flint.

454
Rhea Co., Tenn.

433
Marshall Co., Ky.

515
Henry Co., Tenn.

**Reference:** See Adena.

**Comments:** The examples shown here are Adena-like forms found in Tennessee and western Kentucky. For information on the Tennessee Adena form, see Lewis and Kneberg (1957b). The material is Dover, Tennessee, flint.

**196**
**Ohio**

**Reference:** This example is pictured by Grimm (1953:127). See Robbins Adena.

**Comments:** The material is colorful Ohio Flint Ridge chalcedony.

293, Richland Co., Ohio

365, Montgomery Co., Ky.

788, Ross Co., Ohio

**Reference:** No. 365 is pictured by Thompson (1969). See Robbins Adena.

**Comments:** Many Adena and Hopewell artifacts are found broken or mutilated for reasons not clearly understood. The examples shown here are made from colorful Ohio Flint Ridge chalcedony.

**Reference:** See Robbins Adena and Dickson forms.

**Comments:** This example is marked McPherson Spear and is made from Ohio Flint Ridge material.

148
Preble Co., Ohio
(Lee Mound)

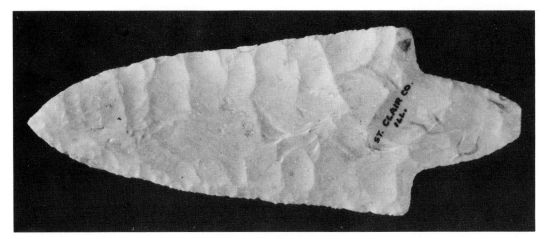

361, St. Clair Co., Ill.

31, Arkansas

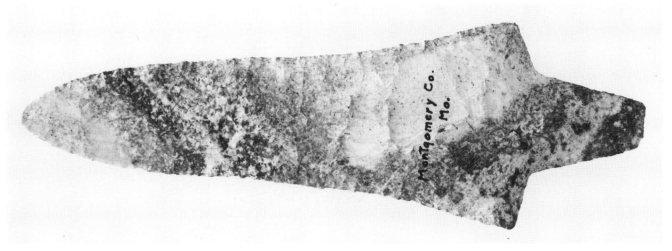

793, Montgomery Co., Mo.

**Reference:** No. 361 is pictured by Perino (1968a). See Dickson (truncated base).

**Comments:** No. 31 is signed J. G. Braeckline, 1940. This example from Arkansas may be a variation of the Dickson.

**Reference:** See Dickson (truncated base).

**Comments:** For information on the Dickson form, see Perino (1968a). The example shown here is made from heat-treated Illinois flint.

303
Rock Island County, Illinois

**524**
**Coweta Co., Ga.**

**Reference:** No data.

**Comments:** Forms similar to the example shown here are found in Florida and sporadically along the Tennessee River Valley west to Arkansas. Examples are found in Tennessee made of white translucent novaculite. This blade is made of amber colored translucent chalcedony.

438

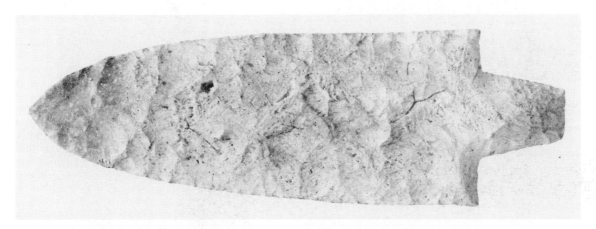

439

458

**Reference:** See Marion, Alachua, Newnan, and others.

**Comments:** For information on this form, see Bullen (1968). The examples shown here are from Flagler County, Florida.

81

**35**
**Tennessee River**

**523**
**Graves Co., Ky.**

**Reference:** No data.

**Comments:** The above examples are similar to Type 16 shown by Webb and DeJarnette (1942, Plate 293). To the author's knowledge, this form has not been named in the southeastern United States.

**Reference:** This example is pictured by Thompson (1984).

**Comments:** Blades with narrow pointed stems of the form shown here are found in Mexico and Central America and are scattered throughout the lower Mississippi River Valley. Similar forms found in Italy are shown by Wilson (1897, Plate 2). The total distribution is not known but it may prove to be extensive. The bi-pointed form may be the widest distributed and may have lasted over a longer period of time than any other form. This example has been ground and polished.

98
Pope Co., Ark.

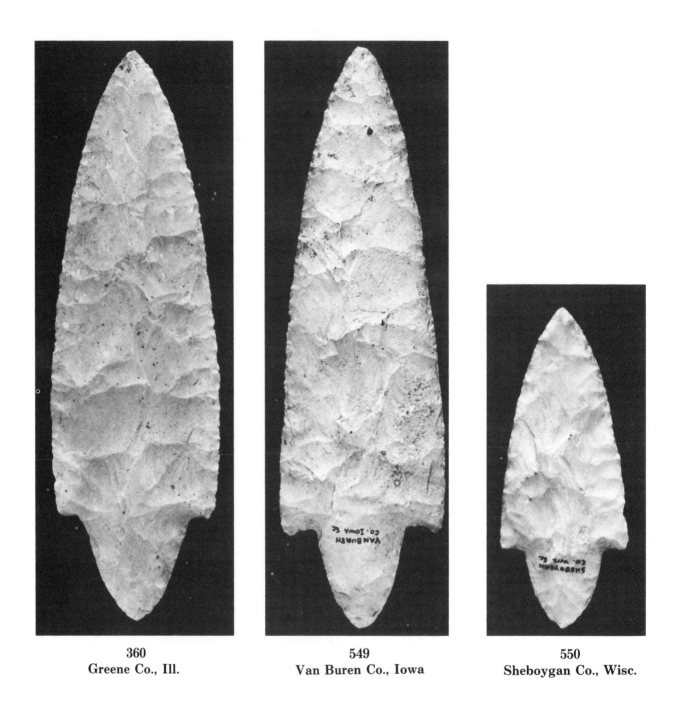

| | | |
|:---:|:---:|:---:|
| 360 | 549 | 550 |
| Greene Co., Ill. | Van Buren Co., Iowa | Sheboygan Co., Wisc. |

**Reference:** See Waubesa and Dickson forms.

**Comments:** Forms identified as Waubesa were made primarily during the Hopewell era and are difficult to separate from the Adena form where the distributional areas overlap.

787
Ohio Co., Ky.

782
Boyle Co., Ky.

434
Lyon Co., Ky.

**Reference:** See Adena, Waubesa, and others.

**Comments:** In the southeastern United States, similar forms are called "beaver-tails." Cultural connections between groups making these forms in the Ohio River Valley and the southeastern United States are not well defined. This form is dominant throughout the Adena Culture and is found in all of the zones of Adena mounds, hence the name Adena (Edler, 1975). The three blades shown here are made from gray Kentucky flint.

724           725           744

**Reference:** No data.

**Comments:** The examples shown here are from a cache of 55 points and were found in Marshall County, Kentucky. To the author's knowledge, this form has not been named in Kentucky.

745           747

**437, Todd Co., Ky.**

**761, Harrison Co., Ind.**

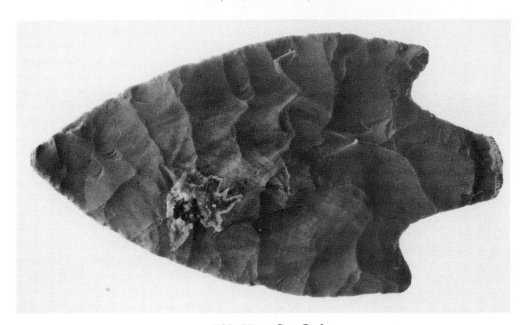

**783, Vigo Co., Ind.**

Reference: No. 761 is pictured by Van Blair (1983a). See Robbins Adena.

**Comments:** This form belongs to the Late Adena manifestation in the Ohio River Valley. For information on the Adena Culture, see Bell (1958).

**Reference:** This example is pictured by Kramer (1947). See Robbins Adena.

**Comments:** This form is often confused with the Harrison Turkey-Tail form.

172
Ohio (County unknown)

**Reference:** See Harrison Turkey-Tail and others.

**Comments:** The examples shown here are different from the classic Harrison Turkey-Tail. In this pattern, the stem edges are ground and the shoulders are wider than those on the Harrison form. Most examples found in western Kentucky and Tennessee were made from material obtained locally. The four examples shown here are from Trigg County, Kentucky, and are a cache.

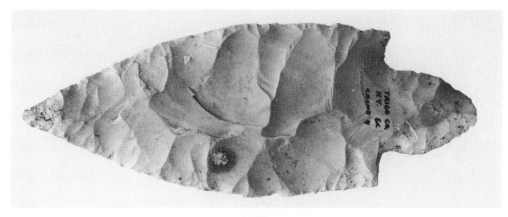

484

483

482

485

460                                        461

**Reference:** These examples are pictured by Knoblock (1948). See Harrison Turkey-Tail (variation).

**Comments:** This form shown here appears to belong to a group of blade patterns having certain features of the Harrison Turkey-Tail. The asymmetry of the blade, such as shown in No. 461, is a consistent feature of the Harrison Turkey-Tail. The examples shown here are from a cache of over 33 blades found in Crawford County, Indiana. To the author's knowledge, this form has not been named in Indiana.

413 412

Crawford Co., Ind.

**Reference:** See data for No. 460 and 461.

**Comments:** These blades are from the same cache. The examples shown here are made from gray Harrison County, Indiana, flint.

464
Pope Co., Ill.

1

2

3

4

Group 870
Arkansas

**Reference:** See Gary.

**Comments:** Group No. 870 represents the typical Gary from Arkansas. Forms similar to No. 464 are found on pre-pottery sites in Arkansas (Ferguson, 1963) and they are believed to be preforms for the Gary (Perino, 1984). This form may be mistaken for the Morrow Mountain, a North Carolina type.

25
Lauderdale Co., Ala.

1            2
Group 733
Tishomingo Co., Miss.

547          548
Tishomingo Co., Miss.

**Reference:** See Morrow Mountain and others.

**Comments:** The name Morrow Mountain identifies a specific form found in Montgomery County, North Carolina. Forms similar to the Morrow Mountain are found in Alabama (Cambron and Hulse, 1975) and in Florida (Bullen, 1968). The total distribution area is not known but the pattern is found over a relatively wide area.

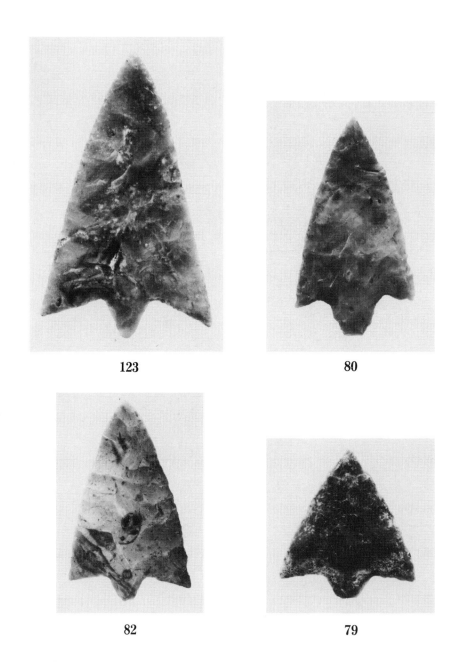

123                    80

82                     79

**Reference:** See Hillsborough.

**Comments:** All of the examples shown are from Hillsborough County, Florida. For information on the Hillsborough form, see Bullen (1968).

849            850            842            852

**Reference:** See Harpeth River and Nuckolls (Dalton).

**Comments:** Similar forms are shown by Guthe (1963). For information on the Harpeth River form, see Cambron and Hulse (1975). The examples shown are from Trigg County, Kentucky.

851

48                              49                              50

**Reference:** See Kirk Stemmed (serrated).

**Comments:** The examples shown here represent the classic Kirk (serrated) form in western Kentucky. The serrations on this form are not a result of resharpening but are constructed as serrations. Occasional examples omit every other point, leaving flat bottom notches between the points producing a harpoon effect. Rare examples are constructed with simple spaced notches in the blade edges producing square barbs with the original contour of the blade remaining from shoulders to tip. These examples are from Stewart County, Tennessee.

537        536        538

**Reference:** See Appalachian Stemmed.

**Comments:** For information on this form, see Kneberg (1957). The examples shown here are made from quartzite. These examples are from Cherokee County, North Carolina.

**643**
**Tishomingo Co., Miss.**

**770**
**Western Kentucky**

**Reference:** No data.

**Comments:** The contracting stem form shown here may represent a common form in use by Archaic groups along the rivers in the eastern United States. It is a common form in western Kentucky and Arkansas eastward to the Pickwick Basin area. The form has been named Elora by Cambron and Hulse (1975) but it has not been named in Arkansas and elsewhere.

**Reference:** See Ledbetter, Maples, Pickwick, Elora, and others.

**Comments:** The example shown here appears to be the same form that was found in shell mound Site Ct°27 by Webb and DeJarnette (1942, Plate 291). In Burial No. 88 at this site were also found blades with the expanded base but without the stem. They are similar to the Bascom Blades (Roshto, 1983) and the Buffalo River Cache from Lewis County, Tennessee (Anderson, 1984). This pattern may be a second stage preform for the types referred to above and others in the Tennessee River Valley.

17
**Lauderdale Co., Ala.**

611                           612                           613

**Reference:** See Ledbetter.

**Comments:** For information on the Ledbetter, see Kneberg (1956) or Cambron and Hulse (1975). These examples are from the distributional area.

472          473          474

**Reference:** See Ledbetter, Maples, Pickwick, Elora, and others.

**Comments:** Type 7 found by Webb and DeJarnette (1942, Plate 158) in shell mound Site Lu°59 in Lauderdale County, Alabama, appears to be the same form as the examples shown here. For information on the Maples form, see Cambron and Hulse (1975). The examples shown here are from Alcorn County, Mississippi.

| 261 | 93 | 898-A | 232 |
| Hempstead Co., Ark. | Pike Co., Ark. | Winkler Co., Texas | |

**Reference:** No. 261 is pictured by LaDassor (1966b). See Scottsbluff, Eden, and Alberta points.

**Comments:** For information on the relationship of the Scottsbluff No. 261 and the Alberta No. 232, see Wormington (1958). Classic examples of the Eden form are shown by Russell (1959). Early collectors referred to these forms with collateral flaking as Collateral Yuma types. This classification was a general category and is no longer used. The Eden and Scottsbluff forms are believed to have been reproduced in recent years.

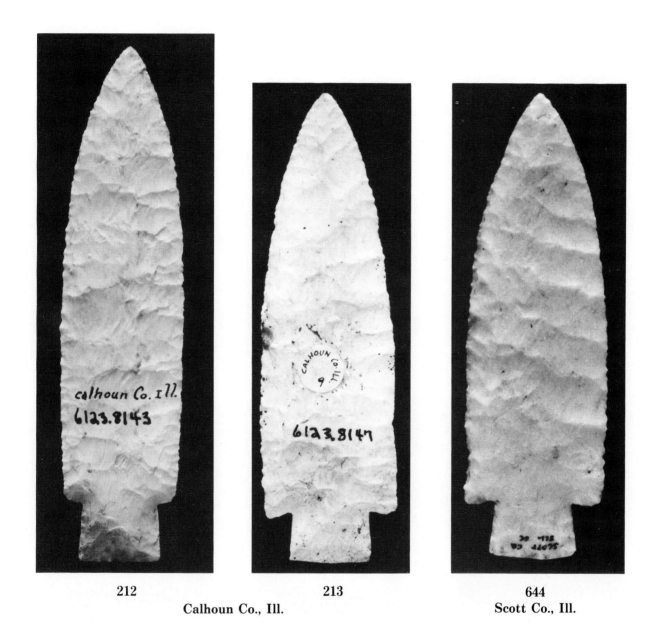

212

213

Calhoun Co., Ill.

644

Scott Co., Ill.

**Reference:** No data.

**Comments:** The examples shown here are not unlike the Scottsbluff Type I described by Wormington (1958:226) except that the shoulders of this form are wider. This form is comparable to the Stemmed Lanceolates described by Converse (1973). Similar forms are called "short-stemmed" Hardins by collectors.

882                    651                    831

**Reference:** See Ohio Lanceolates and Stemmed Lanceolates.

**Comments:** These early points are found together on the same sites (Converse, 1973). The weak shoulders on forms similar to No. 882 are the result of heavy grinding on the stem edges. The examples shown here are made from Ohio Flint Ridge material.

520
Lyon Co., Ky.

508
Lyon Co., Ky.

510
Dickson Co., Tenn.

**Reference:** See Benton (variation).

**Comments:** The cross section of the preform (knife) No. 520 is planoconvex with oblique parallel flaking on the convex side and appears to be the beginning stage of the
leaf-shaped Benton form. No. 510 is the exhausted form. Forms similar to No. 510
have been named Elk River by Cambron and Hulse (1975).

| 260 | 507 | 503 | 509 |
|---|---|---|---|
| | Lyon Co., Ky. | Hart Co., Ky. | Lyon Co., Ky. |

**Reference:** See Benton (variation).

**Comments:** The total distribution of this form is not known but it is found along the Tennessee and Cumberland Rivers in western Kentucky. Examples are found in central Kentucky, the Ohio River Valley in north-central Kentucky, and into Indiana. In Indiana, the stems tend to be longer, tapered toward the base, and better constructed. See Nos. 404 and 685 for examples of the Indiana form.

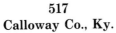

517
Calloway Co., Ky.

504
Benton Co., Tenn.

**Reference:** See Benton (stemmed).

**Comments:** The base of No. 517 represents the classic shape as described by Kneberg (1956). The cross section is often planoconvex with oblique parallel flaking on the convex side only. These features occur frequently on examples from Kentucky and Indiana. The examples shown here may represent an intermediate form.

404
Warrick Co., Ind.

685
Perry Co., Ind.

**Reference:** No. 404 is pictured by LaDassor (1976). See Benton (variation).

**Comments:** The examples shown here from Indiana are almost identical to Kneberg's Benton from Tennessee (1956). In addition to the parallel oblique flaking, both forms are planoconvex in cross section and have almost identical stems. The Indiana forms appear to be somewhat better made and the stems are longer. To the author's knowledge, this form has not been named in Indiana.

602

627

625

**Reference:** See Benton (stemmed).

**Comments:** The large square and round based primary blades found by Webb and DeJarnette (1942) in shell mound context at Site Ct°27 no doubt evolved into many of the named forms found in the Tennessee River Valley. The examples shown here are similar to certain forms described by Lewis and Kneberg from the Eva site in Benton County, Tennessee, (1961, Plate 6). This wide stemmed form has been called Benton Broad Stemmed by Cambron and Hulse (1975). Occasional examples of this wide stemmed form show oblique flaking over random flaking. The examples shown here are from northern Mississippi.

628

109

| 55 | 518 | 519 | 511 |
| Hardin Co., Tenn. | Montgomery Co., Tenn. | Montgomery Co., Tenn. | Stewart Co., Tenn. |

**Reference:** See Elk River and Benton (variation).

**Comments:** The examples shown here are representative of the narrow form with oblique parallel flaking described by Lewis and Kneberg (1961). It is not clear if the stems on some Benton forms were narrowed as the blade was resharpened or if they were made narrow when they were first constructed. No. 511 is probably the exhausted form. For information on the Elk River, see Cambron and Hulse (1975).

**44**
Union Co., Ky.

**514**
Lyon Co., Ky.

**Reference:** See Benton (variation).

**Comments:** The beveling on the blade edges shown here is of the type described by Lewis and Kneberg (1961). The beveling is done by parallel flaking and is often not well controlled. This parallel flaking is one of the identifying features of the type.

516           505           506

**Reference:** No data.

**Comments:** The examples shown here are similar to the forms pictured by Webb and DeJarnette (1942, Plate 101) from Site Lu°25, Unit 1. These examples do not fit precisely into the Benton pattern as described by Kneberg (1956) and may represent simply a flaking technique in use by some of the Archaic groups in the southeastern United States. The examples shown here are from the Tennessee River Valley in northeastern Mississippi.

**180**
**Morrow County, Ohio**

**Reference:** This example is pictured by Kramer (1947) and by Grimm (1953:127). See Ashtabula and "water-point."

**Comments:** This form is made almost exclusively of Plum Run flint. Kramer states that none are known to have been made from Ohio Flint Ridge material. The blade shown here is believed to be the finest example of the form on record.

Obverse                    Reverse

171
Franklin Co., Ohio


Reference: See Ashtabula and "water-point."

Comments: See data for No. 180.

168
LaGrange Co., Ind.

528
Michigan

**Reference:** See Ashtabula and "water-point."

**Comments:** The examples shown here represent the typical shape.

115

529

811
Ross Co., Ohio

814
Pickaway Co., Ohio

**Reference:** See Ashtabula and "water-points".

**Comments:** The examples shown here are typical of the Ashtabula form. See data for No. 180.

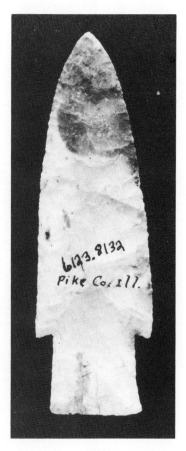

809
Lincoln Co., Mo.

183
Pike Co., Ill.

182
Pike Co., Ill.

**Reference:** No. 809 is pictured by Grimm (1953:87) and by LaDassor (1977). No. 183 is pictured by Perino (1962). See Hardin Barbed forms.

**Comments:** Similar forms are widespread throughout the central and eastern United States. No. 809 is probably one of the finest points known from the St. Louis area.

784
Pike Co., Ill.

903
Hardin Co., Tenn.

**Reference:** No data.

**Comments:** This form is considered by some collectors to be a variation of the Hardin Barbed point. For another example of this form, see Thompson (1971).

118

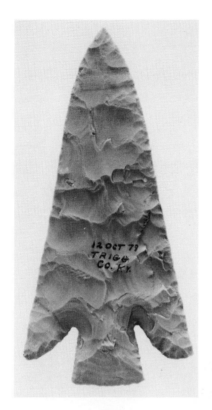

46
Trigg Co., Ky.

47
Trigg Co., Ky.

828
Dearborn Co., Ind.

835
Hardin Co., Ky.

**Reference:** No data is available on the Kentucky forms.

**Comments:** Similar forms found in the Ohio River Valley have been called Buck Creek points (Seeman, 1975). The curvature of the barbs is similar to the Hardin Barbed, Ross (Hopewell), and other forms found in the eastern United States. To the author's knowledge, the Kentucky form has not been named.

491                          629                          492

**Reference:** See Bakers Creek (stemmed Copena).

**Comments:** The Copena and this type probably evolved from the blade forms found by Webb and DeJarnette (1942) in Burial 88 at shell mound Site Ct°27 in Colbert County, Alabama. The stem on this type is similar to some of the Archaic forms found in the area. For information on the Bakers Creek point, see Cambron and Hulse (1975). The examples shown here are from Western Kentucky.

933
Tennessee

743
Benton Co., Tenn.

748
Tennessee

**Reference:** See Cotaco Creek points.

**Comments:** The preform No. 933 shown here is extremely rare and to the author's knowledge, the form has not been shown in any previous publication. No. 743 is from a cache of 54 points found in Benton County, Tennessee, in 1946. All of the points in this cache have rounded tips. Points like No. 748 that have been repointed, presumably for projectile points, have angular tips. The stem and recurved shoulders resemble the Ross (Hopewell) point. Perino (1971a) compares this form with the Snyders. This form is also found in central Kentucky.

**Group 314**
**Miller County, Arkansas**

**Reference:** The two points in the top row are pictured by Bell (1958). See Hayes point.

**Comments:** The examples shown here were found in the northeast part of Mound B, Crenshaw Place and have the designation H-385. For information on the Hayes point, see Bell (1958).

**450**
**Hickman Co., Tenn.**

**451**
**Lawrence Co., Tenn.**

**Reference:** See Pickwick (expanded barb).

**Comments:** The examples shown here are similar to Types 17 and 58 found in shell mound context by Webb and DeJarnette (1942, Plates 158 and 159). This form has many of the characteristics of the Etley type found in the St. Louis, Missouri, area (Titterington, 1950:21). For information on this type in Alabama, see Cambron and Hulse (1975).

763

Hardin Co., Tenn.

**Reference:** See Pickwick (expanded barb).

**416**
**Hardin Co., Tenn.**

**Reference:** See Pickwick (expanded barb).

**117**
Illinois

**382**
Hardin Co., Tenn.

**110**
Independence Co., Ark.

**Reference:** See Buzzard Roost Creek and others.

**Comments:** The examples shown here are similar to Types 30 and 34 found by Webb and DeJarnette (1942, Plate 227) at shell mound Site Lu°67. For information on the Buzzard Roost Creek form, see Cambron and Hulse (1975). To the author's knowledge, the variation No. 117 has not been named.

244
Arkansas (Co. unknown)

97
Pope Co., Ark.

465
Arkansas (Co. unknown)

**Reference:** No data available.

**Comments:** To the author's knowledge, this form has not been named in Arkansas. Material is Ouachita quartzite.

127

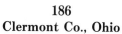

186
Clermont Co., Ohio

185
Ripley Co., Mo.

652
Todd Co., Ky.

**Reference:** See Hardin Barbed and others.

**Comments:** This form was not reported from Ohio by Converse (1973) or Kramer (1947). Similar forms are believed to be variations of the Hardin Barbed type. To the author's knowledge, this form has not been named.

823
Todd Co., Ky.

822

821
Pickaway Co., Ohio

**Reference:** See Heavy-duty point.

**Comments:** For information on the Heavy-duty form, see Edler (1970) and Converse (1973). No. 821 is made from Ohio Flint Ridge material.

88
Georgia
(Flint River)

87
Florida
(Santa Fe River)

**Reference:** See Savannah River point.

**Comments:** For information on the Savannah River point, see Bullen (1968).

190                    192

345                    281                    191
Bastrop Co., Texas     Louisiana


**Reference:** See Pedernales point.

**Comments:** No. 281 is shown here for comparison. For information on the Pedernales form, see Bell (1958).

131

**414**
**Hardin Co., Tenn.**

**19**
**Lauderdale Co., Ala.**

**Reference:** See Benton (stemmed) and Buzzard Roost Creek.

**Comments:** The examples shown are similar to Type 30 found by Webb and DeJarnette (1942, Plate 293) in shell mound context at Site Ct°27. For information on the Buzzard Roost Creek form, see Cambron and Hulse (1975).

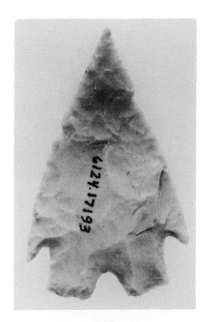

188     344     189

**Bastrop Co., Texas**

**Reference:** See Montell.

**Comments:** For information on the Montell form, see Bell (1958).

**10**
**Morgan Co., Ala.**

**620**
**Tishomingo Co., Miss.**

**621**
**Tishomingo Co., Miss.**

**Reference:** See Fractured Base Stem forms.

**Comments:** Examples of this form are also found in Hardin County, Tennessee. The total distributional area for this form is not known. The basal treatment is characterized by the removal of a single curved flake whose surface is more or less perpendicular to the faces of the blade. To the author's knowledge, this form has not been named.

726          727          728

**Western Kentucky**

353          354          355

**Texas**

**Reference:** Fractured Base Stem forms.

**Comments:** These examples from western Kentucky appear to be variations of the Benton (stemmed) form. See Lewis and Kneberg (1961, Plate 13). To the author's knowledge, this form has not been reported in literature. There is no data available on the Texas form.

178          **Pope Co., Ill.**          179

**Reference:** No. 178 is pictured by Perino (1971a). No. 179 is pictured by Fowler (1951:28) and Grimm (1953:148). See Harrison Turkey-Tail.

**Comments:** The examples shown here are the classic form of the Harrison Turkey-Tail. The blade is usually asymmetrical with one of the notches being lower than the other. The material is generally Harrison County, Indiana, gray flint, but examples may be made from gray Kentucky flint. The gray Indiana and Kentucky flints are difficult to separate.

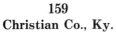

**159**
**Christian Co., Ky.**

**226**
**Marshall Co., Ky.**

**Reference:** No. 226 is pictured by Perino (1971a). See Harrison Turkey-Tail.

**Comments:** The examples shown here are the classic form of the Harrison Turkey-Tail. No. 226 is believed to be one of a cache found near Hardin in Marshall County, Kentucky, many years ago.

309

310

308

**Reference:** These examples are pictured by Grimm (1953:111) and by Bell (1960). See Fulton Turkey-Tail.

**Comments:** Nos. 308 and 309 are the classic Fulton Turkey-Tail. Shown here are three of four points found by Gregory Perino in 1940 near Collinsville, Illinois. The objects pictured on No. 308 and 309 are skeletal finger bones cemented in place by deposited calcite.

**588**
**Hart Co., Ky.**

**772**
**St. Charles Co., Mo.**

**586**
**Franklin Co., Ky.**

**Reference:** See Fulton Turkey-Tail.

**Comments:** These examples represent the classic form of the Fulton Turkey-Tail. Occasional examples show the laminar formation of the nodule from which they were made. When the pattern is in the center of the blade it is called a "bull's-eye" by collectors. Miniature examples of the classic Fulton Turkey-Tail are rare.

139

**Reference:** This example is pictured by Kramer (1947). See Fulton Turkey-Tail.

**Comments:** This form is suggestive of an "end-tanged" knife. Note the "bull's-eye" in the blade. Most examples of the Fulton Turkey-Tail are made from Harrison County, Indiana, or Kentucky gray flint.

161
Ohio

160                                    142

**Reference:** See Fulton Turkey-Tail and variations.

**Comments:** The classic Fulton Turkey-Tail and the small base variation are shown here for comparison. In the author's opinion, the Fulton Turkey-Tail and variations of the form were made as "end-tanged" knives. Exceptional examples of the classic Fulton Turkey-Tail are extremely rare and were probably status symbols since few show any signs of utilitarian use.

387                    388

**Greene County, Indiana**

**Reference:** No. 388 is pictured by Townsend (1939:195). See Fulton Turkey-Tail (variation).

**Comments:** The two blades shown here are from a group of 21 blades found with a red ochre burial.

481, Cherokee Co., N.C.

480, Kentucky (Co. unknown)

667, Graves Co., Ky.

666, Carlisle Co., Ky.

**Reference:** See "end-tanged" knife forms.

**Comments:** For information on "tanged" knives, see Perino (1972).

**290**
**Brown Co., Ill.**

**Reference:** This example is pictured by Knoblock (1939:203), Titterington (1950:29), and Perino (1971a). See Hemphill and Osceola.

**Comments:** This is the original spear found by Ed Hemphill in 1933. The reverse side shown here is encrusted with red ochre stained calcite. In the author's opinion, this is the finest example of the form on record.

Obverse

Reverse

**Reference:** See Hemphill and Osceola.

**Comments:** The Hemphill and Osceola forms are difficult to separate. These forms should be identified on the basis of the archaeological context and distributional area in which they are found. For information on the Old Copper Culture, see Wormington (1958) and Bell (1958).

216
Illinois

457
Missouri

145

146
Cass Co., Ill.

166
Schuyler Co., Ill.

**Reference:** See Hemphill and Osceola.

**Comments:** Same data as for Nos. 216 and 457.

73     70     74

76     75     77

**Reference:** See Bolen Plain and Bolen Beveled.

**Comments:** The Bolen points shown here are both the beveled and unbeveled forms. These examples were found on the Santa Fe River in Florida. For information on the Bolen form, see Bullen (1968).

**526**
Lyon Co., Ky.

**449**
Carlisle Co., Ky.

**475**
Graves Co., Ky.

**Reference:** See Hemphill, Osceola, and Big Sandy.

**Comments:** Typical examples of this notched form from western Kentucky and Tennessee are smaller than the examples shown here and tend to be more narrow in proportion to the length. Occasional examples of the narrow form have parallel flaking and a median ridge. No. 449 appears to be the shape before resharpening. To the author's knowledge, this form has not been named in Kentucky.

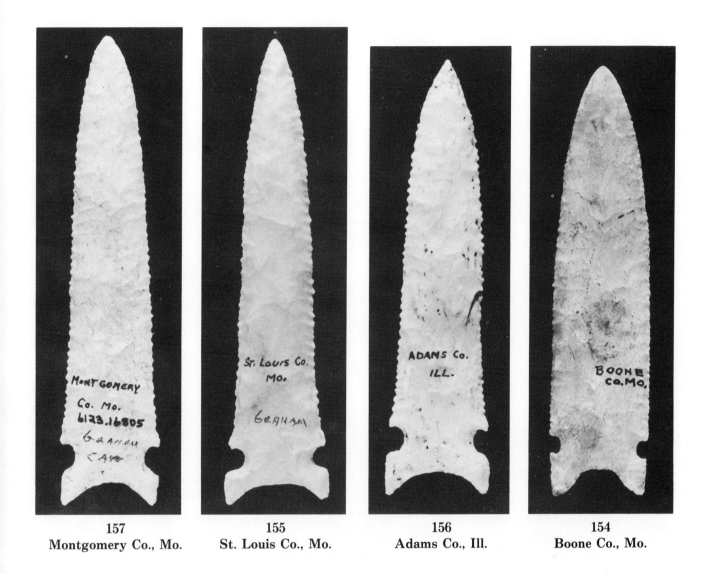

| 157 | 155 | 156 | 154 |
| Montgomery Co., Mo. | St. Louis Co., Mo. | Adams Co., Ill. | Boone Co., Mo. |

**Reference:** Nos. 155, 156, and 157 are pictured by Perino (1968a). No. 157 is also pictured by Perino (1962). See Graham Cave Side Notch.

**Comments:** This form is similar to the Hemphill, Osceola, Big Sandy, Cache River, and others. For information on the Graham Cave Side Notch, see Logan (1952:28).

| 1 | 2 | 1 | 2 |
|---|---|---|---|
| Rankin Co., Miss. | Hinds Co., Miss. | Madison Co., Miss. | Rankin Co., Miss. |

Group 920

Group 922

**Reference:** See Cache River, Big Sandy, and others.

**Comments:** The Mississippi and Arkansas Cache River forms are shown here for comparison. No. 104 is a fine example of the Arkansas Cache River form as described by Cloud (1969).

104

**174**
**Mayes Co., Okla.**

**Reference:** This blade is pictured by Perino (1970a).

**Comments:** The blade is from a cache of four found near Salina, Oklahoma. Perino states that the four blades are made from gray-colored Barren Fork flint and are thought to have been made in the early Spiro Phase. The four blades in the cache range from 10½″ to 14½″ in length. The blade shown here is actual size.

**Reference:** See Little River point.

**Comments:** For examples of the Little River point, see Wilson (1897, Plate 61). Wilson shows a group of five blades from a cache of 14 found on the Little Missouri River in Arkansas. The sizes of the blades shown in this cache ranged from 11″ down and appear to be made from novaculite.

26
**Mississippi Co., Ark.**

**334**
**McCurtain County, Okla.**

**Reference:** This example is pictured by Perino (1976c). See Little River point.

**Comments:** The example shown here is probably the shape of the form before resharpening. This example is made from white novaculite.

43
Pope County, Ark.


**Reference:** See Little River point.

**Comments:** See data for No. 26. This form may have been reproduced in recent years.

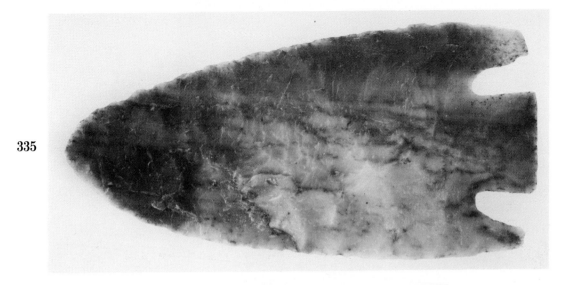

335

336

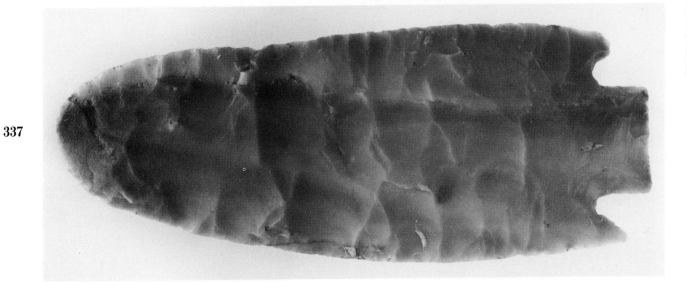

337

**Reference:** These examples are pictured by Perino (1976a). See Little River points.

**Comments:** The three blades shown here are from a cache of five found by Dorothy Perino in McCurtain County, Oklahoma, in 1976. The material is novaculite.

362, St. Charles Co., Mo.

227, Lincoln Co., Mo.

187, St. Clair Co., Ill.

273, Adams Co., Ill.

**Reference:** No. 362 is pictured by Grimm (1953:71). See Etley and Smith.

**Comments:** The typical Etley has shorter barbs than the form shown here. The form No. 362 has been named Mehlville by Perino (1983). No. 273 is polished on the reverse side.

61   56   59

66   67   65

**Reference:** See Citrus and Hernando.

**Comments:** Bullen (1968) states that, "Citrus points are associated with Hernando points and may be the knife form of the same complex." The two forms are shown here for comparison. Nos. 56, 59, and 61 are from Pasco County, Florida, and are representative of the Citrus form. Nos. 65, 66, and 67 are from Hillsborough County, Florida, and are representative of the Hernando form.

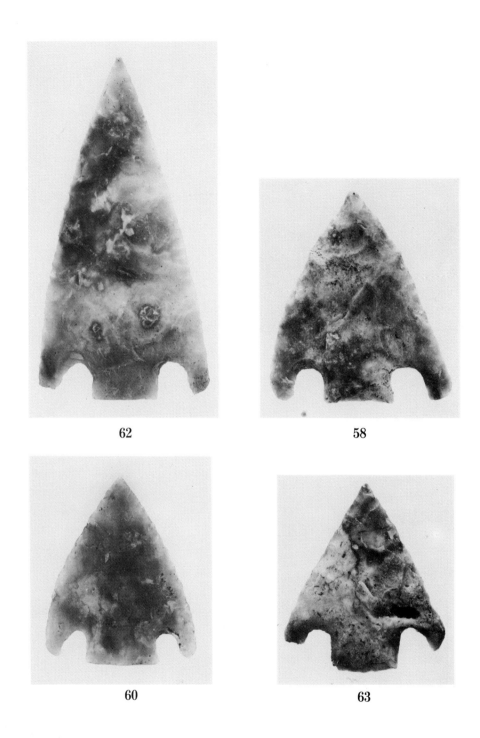

62                 58

60                 63

**Reference:** Nos. 60, 62, and 63 are pictured by Van Blair (1982b). See Culbreath.

**Comments:** Nos. 58 and 63 are from Pasco County, Florida. Nos. 60 and 62 are from Hillsborough County, Florida. For information on the Culbreath, see Bullen (1968).

441
Dickson Co., Tenn.

703
Stewart Co., Tenn.

440
Alcorn Co., Miss.

**Reference**: See Lost Lake and "deep-notch".

**Comments**: The examples shown here are the typical shapes of the "deep-notched" forms from the Tennessee and Cumberland River areas. For information on the Lost Lake form, see Cambron and Hulse (1975).

584
Pickett Co., Tenn.

758
Hardin Co., Tenn.

372
Clark Co., Ky.

779
Hart Co., Ky.

373
Posey Co., Ind.

**Reference:** Nos. 372 and 373 are pictured by LaDassor (1958a). No. 372 is also pictured by Thompson (1971a). No. 779 is pictured by LaDassor (1977). See Lost Lake and "deep-notch".

**Comments:** Note the similarity between these examples and the Tennessee and Cumberland River Valley forms.

805
Bourbon Co., Ky.

825
Barren Co., Ky.

698
Ohio Co., Ky.

702
Martin Co., Ind.

**Reference:** See Lost Lake and "deep-notch".

**Comments:** No. 805 is probably the shape of this notched form before resharpening. Note the serrations on the lower part of the blade of No. 659.

659
Hart Co., Ky.

640
Todd Co., Ky.

486
Kentucky

**Reference:** See Lost Lake and "deep-notch".

**Comments:** The examples shown here are tentatively identified as a variation of the Lost Lake form. The notches appear to be more shallow and the blade is not usually resharpened by beveling as in the typical Lost Lake.

**442**
**Montgomery Co., Tenn.**

**656**
**Ohio**

**443**
**Cherokee Co., N.C.**

**444**
**Tennessee**

**Reference:** See Ohio Notched Base Dovetail.

**Comments:** The examples shown here appear to be more like the Lost Lake "deep-notch" than the "dove-tail". The notch in the center of the base is one of the identifying features of this form. For information on this form, see Converse (1973).

597
Lawrence Co., Tenn.

494

487

**Reference:** No data.

**Comments:** The angle of the notches with the longitudinal axis of the blade in this form is less than that of the St. Charles "dove-tail" but greater than that of the average Lost Lake "deep-notch" form. To the author's knowledge, this notched form has not been named.

164

**760**
**Jefferson Co., Ky.**

**583**
**Hart Co., Ky.**

**759**
**Spencer Co., Ind.**

**585**
**Hart Co., Ky.**

**Reference:** Nos. 759 and 760 are pictured by Van Blair (1983a). See Lost Lake and "deep-notch".

**Comments:** The examples shown here are serrated by beveling the edge on both faces of the blade. This beveling produces a flat-hexagonal cross section. This technique of serrating the blade edges is extremely rare in the Lost Lake "deep-notch" form. To the author's knowledge, this form has not been named.

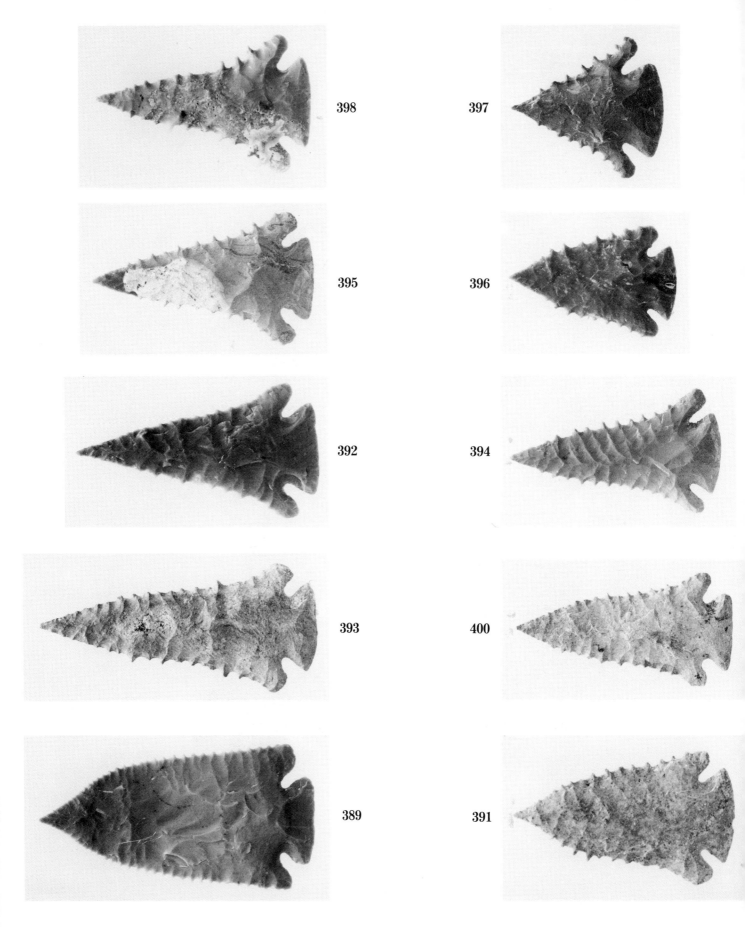

398

397

395

396

392

394

393

400

389

391

**Reference:** No. 389 is pictured by Van Blair (1981). See Pine Tree points.

**Comments:** The examples shown here are from Harrison County, Indiana.

**522**
**Putnam Co., Tenn.**

**513**
**Putnam Co., Tenn.**

**415**
**Alabama**

**Reference:** Similar forms from Davidson County, Tennessee, are pictured by Thompson (1970).

**Comments:** Almost identical forms were found by Webb and DeJarnette (1942, Plate 291) in Burial No. 88, shell mound Site Ct°27, in Colbert County, Alabama. Provisional Type 2-Expanded Stem described by Cambron and Hulse (1975) has similar features. To the author's knowledge, this form has not been named.

202

284

285

283

**Reference:** Nos. 283 and 284 are pictured by Bell (1958). See Afton points.

**Comments:** The examples shown here are from Missouri and Arkansas and represent some of the variations within the Afton form. The notched forms may have a slightly incurvate to slightly excurvate basal edge while the stemmed form may have the shoulders removed.

Group 340                                    Group 341

Red River Co., Texas

**Reference:** See Morris point.

**Comments:** These examples were found at the Dan Holdeman Site near Idabel, Oklahoma. Perino (1983) suggests that there is some variation in the Morris form, at least on a local basis. For information on the Morris point, see Bell (1958).

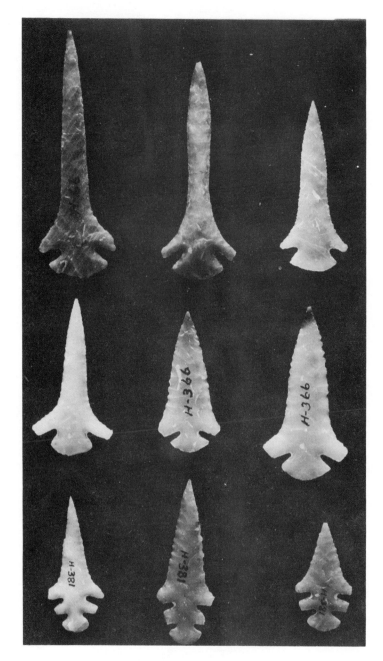

**Group 203**
**Miller County, Arkansas**

**Reference:** The first point in the top row and the three points in the bottom row are pictured by Perino (1968a). See Agee points.

**Comments:** These examples are from the Crenshaw Site.

**173**
**Ross County, Ohio**

**Reference:** This blade is pictured by Grimm (1953:144) and by Perino (1968a). See Ross (Hopewell).

**Comments:** This outstanding artifact was excavated in 1891-92 by W. K. Moorehead from Hopewell Mound 25 in Ross County, Ohio. The material is obsidian.

**Reference:** This blade is pictured by Grimm (1953:115). See Ross (Hopewell).

**Comments:** The notched and unnotched Ross blades are found together in Hopewell mortuary offerings. The material is obsidian.

**215**
**Ross County, Ohio**

**774**
**Calhoun Co., Ill.**

**Reference:** This example is pictured by Knoblock (1955) and by LaDassor (1974). See Ross (Hopewell).

**Comments:** This example was found broken. Many Hopewell artifacts, probably owned by status individuals, are found broken or mutilated. It is the author's guess that this was done in some cases to discourage grave robbers. This Ross (Hopewell) blade is probably the finest on record made of Knife River flint.

**316**
**Montgomery Co., Mo.**

**Reference:** See Ross (Hopewell).

**Comments:** The example shown here is the same form as No. 173. The stem is out of type but the termination of the shoulders is diagnostic of the form. This example is made of Kaolin flint.

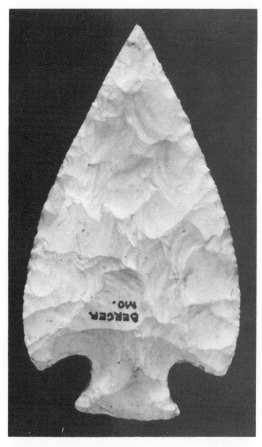

775, Berger, Mo.                    165, Calhoun Co., Ill.

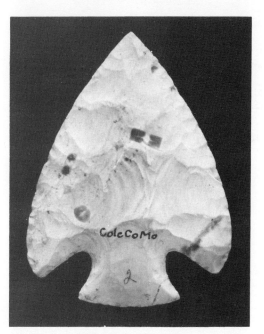

777, Cooper Co., Mo.                776, Cole Co., Mo.

**Reference:** No. 775 is pictured by Grimm (1953:43). Nos. 776 and 777 are pictured by Baldwin (1979a). See Snyders point.

**Comments:** No. 165 was found at the Snyders Site, Calhoun County, Illinois, and is the classic form of the Snyders point. Fake Snyders points have been made from genuine North Points, or North Blades, in recent years.

**Reference:** This blade is pictured by Fowler (1951:28) and Young (1910). See St. Charles and "dove-tail".

**Comments:** The example shown here is believed to be the finest gray "dove-tail" found in Kentucky. This truncated stem form, to the author's knowledge, has not been named in Kentucky.

177
**Warren Co., Ky.**

**471, Barren Co., Ky.**

**408, Williamson Co., Ill.**

**489, Hardin Co., Ky.**

789, Mercer Co., Ky.

**Reference:** No. 789 is pictured by Webb and Funkhouser (1928:213). Nos. 789 and 408 are pictured by Baldwin (1980). See St. Charles and "dove-tail".

**Comments:** These examples are the truncated stem form. Note the "bull's-eye" in No. 408 and the "clipped" barbs of No. 471.

**608, Illinois**

**655, Ohio**

**610, Calhoun Co., Ill.**

**607, LaSalle Co., Ill.**

**609, Boone Co., Mo.**

**Reference:** See St. Charles and "dove-tail".

**Comments:** This pattern is found in the Ohio River Valley west into Illinois and Missouri. The notches in this type tend to be more open and more shallow than the truncated stem form.

178

**798**
**Dunklin Co., Mo.**

**799**
**Mercer Co., Ky.**

**653**
**Ohio**

**Reference:** No. 798 is pictured by McPherson (1963). No. 799 is pictured by LaDassor (1958b). See St. Charles and "dove-tail".

**Comments:** The examples shown here have a slight indentation of the basal edge and are a variation of the truncated stem form. The beveling on the right edges of the blade on No. 798 is an extremely rare feature in the "dove-tail" form.

| 406 | 498 | 499 |
| Grayson Co., Ky. | Hardin Co., Tenn. | Hart Co., Ky. |

**Reference:** See St. Charles and "dove-tail".

**Comments:** These examples have a slight indentation of the basal edge and are a variation of the truncated stem form. The serrated form No. 406 is rare and is similar to the fractured base "dove-tail" (Converse, 1973).

| 478 | 477 | 479 |
| Graves Co., Ky. | Montgomery Co., Tenn. | Graves Co., Ky. |

**Reference:** See St. Charles and "dove-tail".

**Comments:** The faces of the blade on this form tend to be flat and the beveling produces a rhomboid cross-section. To the author's knowledge, this form has not been named.

496
Ohio Co., Ky.

495
Kentucky

500
Indiana

501

**Reference:** No data.

**Comments:** The angle of the notches with the longitudinal axis of the blade in this form is less than that of the St. Charles "dove-tail" but greater than the average Lost Lake form. This form has been called "notched base dove-tail" by collectors.

182

302
Tennessee

**Reference:** This blade is pictured by LaDassor (1966b). See St. Charles and "dove-tail".

**Comments:** This example appears to be a variation of the truncated stem form. The large indentation in the base gives the stem a lobed appearance. Similar types are found in Kentucky. To the author's knowledge, this lobed form has not been named in Kentucky or Tennessee.

**169**
**Greene Co., Ohio**

**Reference:** This example is pictured by Grimm (1953:123). See St. Charles and "dove-tail".

**Comments:** This blade is called the Oldtown Spear. The material is Ohio Flint Ridge translucent chalcedony. In the author's opinion, this is one of the finest small base "dove-tails" on record.

242
Miami County, Ohio

**Reference:** This example is pictured by Grimm (1953:123). See St. Charles and "dove-tail".

**Comments:** The blade shown here is called the Sears Spear. The material is Ohio Flint Ridge chalcedony.

231
Ohio

**Reference:** See St. Charles and "dove-tail".

**Comments:** The blade shown here is marked No. 8, Chas. Eicher, Ohio. The material is Ohio Flint Ridge chalcedony.

**149**
**Darke Co., Ohio**

**Reference:** See St. Charles and "dove-tail".

**Comments:** This blade is made from Ohio Flint Ridge chalcedony.

263
Delaware Co., Ohio

147
Franklin Co., Ohio

150
Greene Co., Ohio

**Reference:** See St. Charles and "dove-tail".

**Comments:** No. 263 is marked The Hill Spear, No. 147 is marked The Lisle Spear, and No. 150 is marked the Bunch Spear. All are made from Ohio Flint Ridge chalcedony.

**301**
**Clark Co., Ark.**

**Reference:** This example is pictured by LaDassor (1966b). See St. Charles and "dove-tail".

**Comments:** For information on the St. Charles, see Bell (1960).

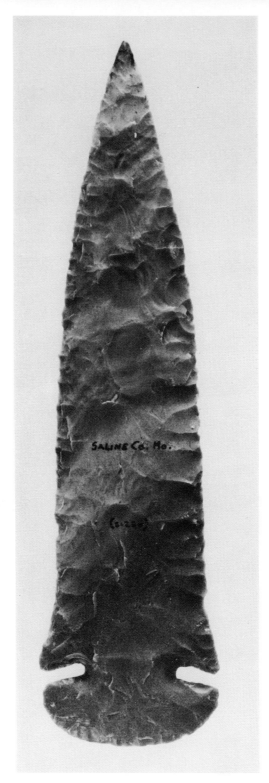

**170**
Saline Co., Mo.

**Reference:** This example is pictured by LaDassor (1966b). See St. Charles and "dove-tail".

**Comments:** Exceptional examples of the type shown here are very rare and this blade is among the finest known. Typical examples are made from white flint.

**469**
Lawrence Co., Tenn.

**686**
Marshall Co., Ky.

**470**
Hart Co., Ky.

**Reference:** See St. Charles and "dove-tail".

**Comments:** These examples show similarities between the Kentucky and Tennessee forms.

**688**
**Hardin Co., Tenn.**

**490**
**Wayne Co., Tenn.**

**Reference:** See Plevna, St. Charles, and "dove-tail".

**Comments:** Points with beveled edges and rounded bases similar to the examples shown here have been called Plevna by Cambron and Hulse (1975).

195
Texas

210
Llano Co., Texas

**Reference:** No. 210 is pictured by Patterson (1936). See "corner-tang" knife.

**Comments:** These two blades were in the J. T. Patterson collection. This type of blade is believed to have been reproduced in recent years.

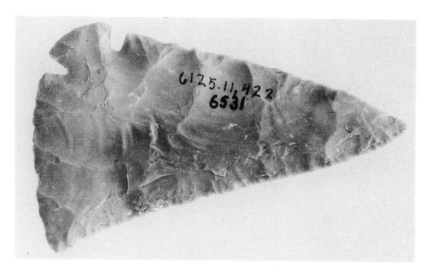

199, Texas

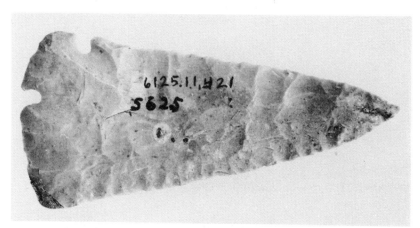

200, Bastrop County, Texas

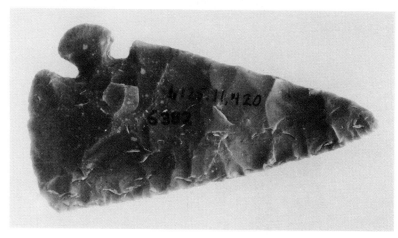

198, Texas

**Reference:** No. 200 is pictured by Patterson (1936). See ''corner-tang'' knife.

**Comments:** These three blades were in the J. T. Patterson collection.

307
LeFlore Co., Okla.

**Reference:** This example is pictured by Perino (1967b). See Kay Blade.

**Comments:** Perino states that the blade shown here is one of six found at Spiro Mound in LeFlore County, Oklahoma. It is made from Kay County, Oklahoma, flint and is known as the Kay Blade.

Flint Ridge Chalcedony Spear.
— Miami University Museum —
— Oxford Ohio —

75

## 262
### Butler Co., Ohio

**Reference:** This blade is pictured by Grimm (1953:114).

**Comments:** This blade is called the Butler County Spear. The material is Ohio Flint Ridge chalcedony.

**Group 204**
**Yell County, Arkansas**

**Reference:** See Keota points.

**Comments:** These examples are marked H-478. For information on the Keota point, see Perino (1968a).

**11**
**Hardin Co., Tenn.**

**757**
**Wayne Co., Tenn.**

**720**
**Hardin Co., Tenn.**

**Reference:** No. 11 is pictured by Van Blair (1982c). See Pine Tree.

**Comments:** No. 11 shown here is the classic Pine Tree. The form is shown by Perino (1968a). The notches are typically shallow but they are narrow and well developed as in the Lost Lake and "deep-notched" forms. It has some similarity to the Kirk Corner Notched points found by Broyles (1971) at the Hardaway and Doershuk sites in North Carolina. The typical Pine Tree point may be a resharpened wider point. This point is rare and there are few classic examples known.

| 826 | 366 | 598 |
|:---:|:---:|:---:|
| Logan Co., Ky. | Brown Co., Ohio | Lawrence Co., Tenn. |

**Reference:** No. 366 is pictured by Duncan (1973b:149). See Lost Lake and "deep-notch".

**Comments:** These eared base points are shown for comparison. No. 366 is made from Ohio Flint Ridge material. To the author's knowledge, the forms have not been named.

445, Hardin Co., Ky.

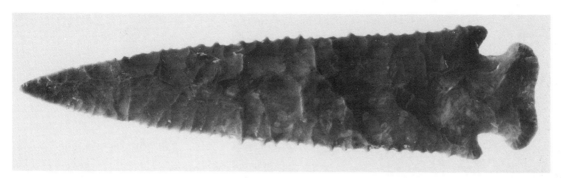

773, Boyle Co., Ky.

797
Boyle Co., Ky.

792, Grayson Co., Ky.

225, Ohio (County unknown)

Reference: See "Knobbed-Hardin".

Comments: It appears that this type is a resharpened wider form.

200

639                 638             637
Perry Co., Tenn.

**Reference:** No data.

**Comments:** Nos. 638 and 639 are from the Tennessee River Valley in northeastern Mississippi. No. 637 is similar to the Thebes form found in Illinois, Indiana, and Ohio areas. To the author's knowledge, this form has not been named.

829
Carlisle Co., Ky.

54
Lauderdale Co., Ala.

836
Hart Co., Ky.

840
White Co., Tenn.

837
Hart Co., Ky.

596
Hart Co., Ky.

839
White Co., Tenn.

**Reference:** No. 54 is pictured by Wilkes (1982). See LeCroy and Rice (Lobed).

**Comments:** No. 54 is a classic example of the eastern form. Nos. 839 and 840 are typical examples of the LeCroy type. For information on the LeCroy type, see Kneberg (1956).

**603**
**Graves Co., Ky.**

**717**

**718**

**Reference:** No data.

**Comments:** Nos. 717 and 718 are also from western Kentucky. The form is found sporadically from western to central Kentucky but examples are rare. It is characterized by the removal of a conchoidal flake from the center of the basal edge on one or both sides of the blade. Sometimes the flake hinges out, giving the appearance of a shallow flute. The lobed basal corners and the shallow notches are identifying features of the form. A similar type is found in southwestern Missouri but the notches are two to three times as deep. No. 718 is a classic example of the form. To the author's knowledge, this form has not been named in Kentucky.

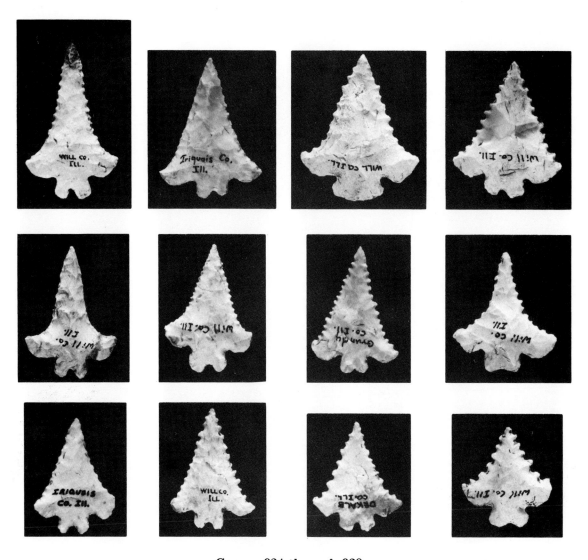

**Groups 924 through 928**

**Reference:** See Fox Valley and "clipped-wing".

**Comments:** The examples shown here represent the typical forms of the Fox Valley as illustrated by DeCamp (1967). For information on the Fox Valley form, see Perino (1971a).

**456**
**Cass Co., Ill.**

**Reference:** See Stilwell.

**Comments:** The example shown here, found in the type area, may represent the shape of the Stilwell as it looked before resharpening. (Of special interest is the collector ownership sequence of this particular piece. The markings and labels begin with the first owner, J. G. Braecklein of Kansas City, Missouri, indicated by the script showing location and date of find. Braecklein was one of the purchasing agents for Edward Payne of Springfield, Illinois, who assembled one of the largest private collections in North America. The piece then went to B. W. Stevens of Quincy, Illinois, who in turn conveyed it to Dr. T. Hugh Young of Nashville, Tennessee, as indicated by the label bearing the letter "S". Subsequently the piece went to E. E. Curtiss, Sr., as indicated by the label bearing the initials "EC" in script. Many collectors marked their material in the early days but one should be extremely careful in accepting labels as a guarantee of authenticity since some of the markings of the "old time" collectors have been faked).

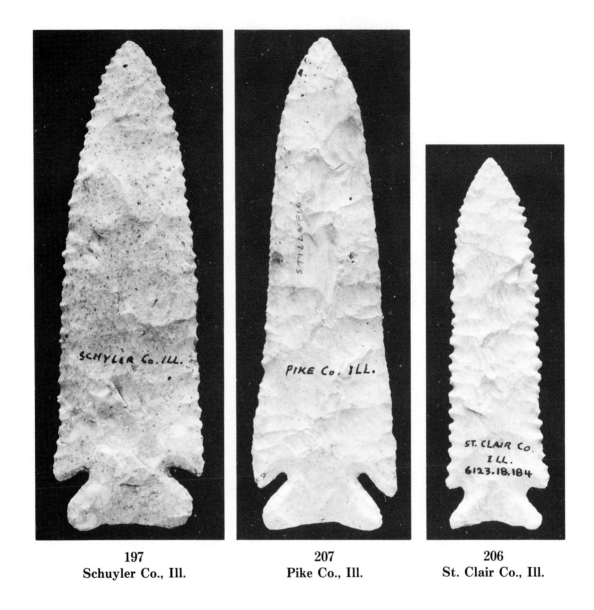

197
Schuyler Co., Ill.

207
Pike Co., Ill.

206
St. Clair Co., Ill.

**Reference:** No. 206 is pictured by Thompson (1970) and Perino (1971a). See Stilwell.

**Comments:** The examples shown here represent the typical resharpened form. For information on the Stilwell, see Perino (1970b).

**929, Illinois (County unknown)**

**274, Brown Co., Ill.**

**930, Illinois
(County unknown)**

**Reference:** No. 274 is pictured by Perino (1971a). See Thebes.

**Comments:** Typical notches shown here are squared at the end but in some examples they are rounded. If the blade is resharpened, it is usually done by beveling.

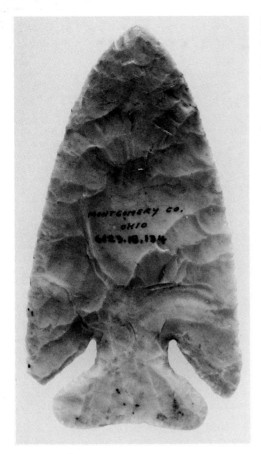

271
Montgomery Co., Ohio

579
Ohio

578
Ohio

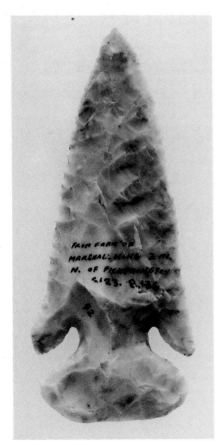

270
Fairfield Co., Ohio

269
Ohio

**Reference:** See Thebes (variation).

**Comments:** The notches on this form curve upward resulting in a slightly longer stem than the Thebes (Perino, 1971a). Note the variation in the examples shown here. The material is Ohio Flint Ridge chalcedony.

  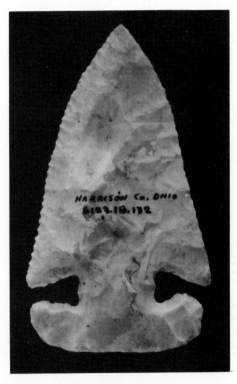

377
Preble County, Ohio

249
Richland Co., Ohio

272
Harrison Co., Ohio

**Reference:** See Thebes and "E" notched points.

**Comments:** The three examples shown here are made from Ohio Flint Ridge material. Note the "lightning" streak in the base of No. 249. This form is a variation of the Thebes point (Perino, 1971a). For information on Ohio Flint Ridge material, see Holmes (1919) and Kramer (1947).

781
Adams Co., Ohio

780
Pickaway Co., Ohio

819
Ross Co., Ohio

813
Licking Co., Ohio

818
Pickaway Co., Ohio

**Reference:** See Decatur and "fractured-base" points.

**Comments:** No. 780 is named the Logan Elm point. No. 813 is similar to the Afton form from Missouri and Ohio, described by Bell (1958). Afton-like points of this type with fractured bases are extremely rare. For information on the "fractured-base" forms from Ohio, see Converse (1973).

795
Mercer Co., Ky.

448
Western Kentucky

865
Todd Co., Ky.

862
Hart Co., Ky.

1

2

Group 867
Western Kentucky

**Reference:** See Decatur and "fractured-base" points.

**Comments:** The Kentucky examples shown here tend to be more like the forms found in Indiana and Ohio than those described by Cambron and Hulse (1975) from Alabama. Like the Ohio forms described by Converse (1973), the forms shown here are seldom beveled.

**765**
**Colbert Co., Ala.**

**766**
**Lawrence Co., Ala.**

**767**
**Lauderdale Co., Ala.**

**2**

**6**

**7**

**Group 531**

**Group 734**

**Tishomingo Co., Miss.**

**Reference:** See Decatur and "fractured-base" points.

**Comments:** For information on the Decatur form, see Bell (1960) and Cambron and Hulse (1975). The examples shown here represent the typical form of the Decatur as described by Cambron. In the author's opinion, this form is a resharpened version of a wider blade.

5       3a       3b       6

1       4b       9       4a

Group 531: Nos. 3a and 4a

Group 734: Nos. 1, 3b, 4b, 5, 6, and 9

**Reference:** See Decatur and "fractured-base" points.

**Comments:** The fracturing of the base in the form shown here is not well developed. Small flakes are taken off only on the corners of the base. These forms have a notched or concave base. In the better developed examples of the "fractured-base" form, this notched or concave base facilitated the fracturing of the stem by allowing the removal of two short flakes. In some examples, a single flake followed the curve in the base. Other examples have two flakes terminating in the center of the base forming a shallow vee. In the highly developed forms, a single flat or slightly curved flake was taken off across the entire base and often terminated with the removal of a small flake down the side of the stem. Rare examples show a small notch in the center of the base. The examples shown here are from the Pickwick Basin area of northeastern Mississippi.

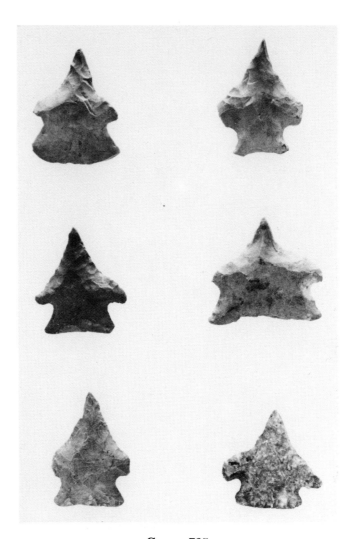

**Group 735**

**Reference:** See Chisel Point Graver.

**Comments:** This form is characterized by the removal of a single flake on each side of the point. These two flakes create an angular chisel-like tip. The examples shown here also have a flake taken off on each corner of the stem, similar to the "fractured-base" forms found in the same area. These examples are from the Pickwick Basin area of northeastern Mississippi.

614
Indiana

796
Christian Co., Ky.

615
Lyon Co., Ky.

618
Warren Co., Ky.

617
Henry Co., Tenn.

616
Carlisle Co., Ky.

**Reference:** See Fractured Base Dove-Tail.

**Comments:** Two patterns are shown here. Of the round base forms, the "clipped-wing" No. 796 is the most rare. For information on this form, see Converse (1973).

711
Alcorn Co., Miss.

712

715

710

709

713

Reference: See "fractured-base" notched form.

Comments: The flake removed from the base is the same as the stemmed form but the base is notched more like the Eva point. The Kirk-like and Eva-like forms are found on the same sites in western Kentucky. Similar forms are shown by Lewis and Kneberg (1961, Plate 8) but no reference is made by them to any unusual flaking of the base. All of the examples shown except No. 711 are from Marshall County, Kentucky.

378                                   381

**Stewart Co., Tenn.**

Reference: No. 378 is pictured by Thompson (1968, 1984:35).

Comments: These barbed daggers, or spear points, are from the Mississippian Cultural Period and may have been ritual paraphernalia. The author has encountered six variations of this form.

**707**
**Crittenden Co., Ark.**

**Reference:** See Caddo blades.

**Comments:** These Caddo blades, because of their size and quality of workmanship, were probably Mississippian ritual paraphernalia. For similar forms, see "The Kizzia Blades" (Kizzia, 1968).

**708**
**Pike Co., Ark.**

**Reference:** See Caddo serrated knife (ceremonial dance sword).

**Comments:** For information on the Ceremonial Complex of Etowah (Georgia), Moundville (Alabama), and Spiro (Oklahoma), see Fundaburk and Foreman (1957). Large blades of this form are believed to have been reproduced in recent years.

379
Stewart Co., Tenn.

677
Humphreys Co., Tenn.

**Reference:** No. 379 is pictured by Thompson (1984:35). See Flint Sword.

**Comments:** Parallel sided blades with rounded bases and "rat-tail" tips similar to the examples shown here are known with a length of 27½". For a description of this form, see Fundaburk and Foreman (1957, Plate 91). This form has been reproduced in recent years.

220

671
Obion Co., Tenn.

678
Dickson Co., Tenn.

**Reference:** No data.

**Comments:** The blade forms shown here from Tennessee are unusual. Other examples of form No. 671 are known to the author but typical examples are smaller and are not as well made as the one shown here. To the author's knowledge, the form No. 678 has not been reported in literature from Tennessee.

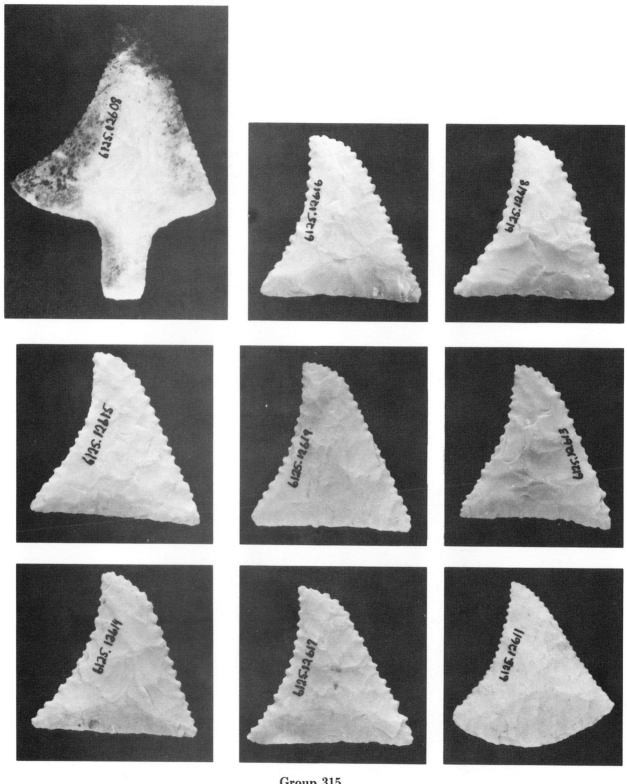

**Group 315**
**(Cahokia Mounds)**
**Madison Co., Ill.**

**Reference:** Three of these examples are pictured by Perino (1985b:61). See flint Cahokia Sharkstooth.

**Comments:** These flint sharks teeth replicas are Mississippian ritual paraphernalia and are extremely rare and unique in North American archaeology. They have been found only in the Cahokia Mound group. These examples were found by Gregory Perino in a burial near Monks Mound, along with the remnants of a wooden club in which they were apparently mounted.

655

653

656

654

**Reference:** See Upper Mercer, Coshocton, and other Ohio black flint.

**Comments:** This black flint and other colorful materials, such as the Flint Ridge chalcedony, from Ohio is very desirable and blades and projectile points made from it are highly sought by collectors. Reproductions have been made from these colorful materials in recent years.

296                                        297

**Reference:** Both of these examples are pictured by Perino (1962).

**Comments:** Perino states that these forms are Hopewell blades of a rare type found in the Mississippi Valley. Forms similar to No. 296 are found in the Kentucky Lake area of western Kentucky and Tennessee. This pattern is distinctly different from the Copena type. The examples shown here were found in or near Klunk Mound 6 in Calhoun County, Illinois.

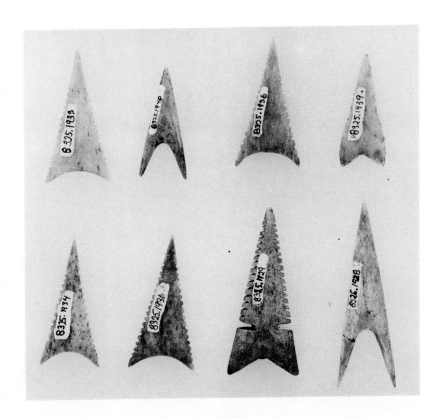

**Group 313**
**(Cahokia site)**

**Reference:** The third point from the left in the bottom row is pictured by Perino (1947). See Cahokia points.

**Comments:** Bone points of this type are extremely rare. The examples shown here were found at Cahokia sites in St. Clair and Madison Counties in Illinois.

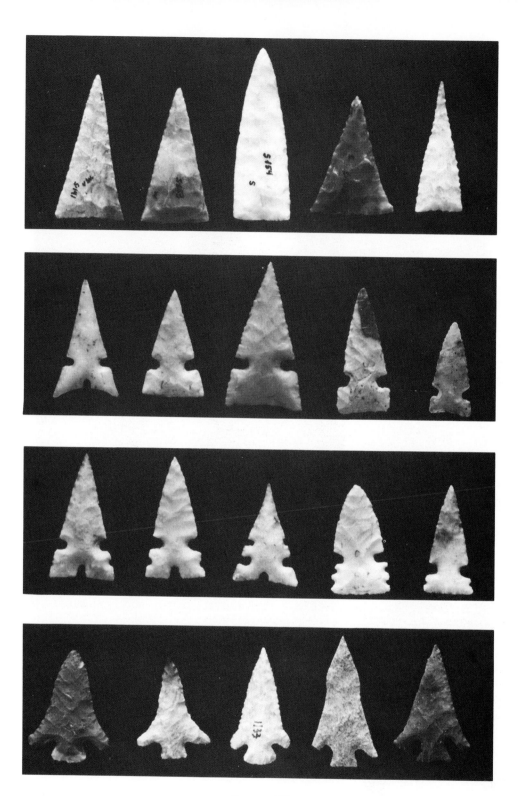

**Group 428**
**(Cahokia site)**

**Reference:** See Cahokia Gem Points.

**Comments:** The examples shown here are from Cahokia sites in St. Clair and Madison Counties in Illinois and are representative of the different notched and unnotched forms pictured by Titterington (1938). Some of the forms pictured by Titterington have been renamed for other locations.

**657**
**Illinois**

**247**
**St. Louis Co., Mo.**

**248**
**St. Charles Co., Mo.**

**342**
**Pike Co., Ill.**

**Reference:** No. 248 is pictured by Perino (1971a).

**Comments:** No. 248 has been called "eared" Scottsbluff. These examples represent some of the unusual point forms from the Missouri and Illinois areas.

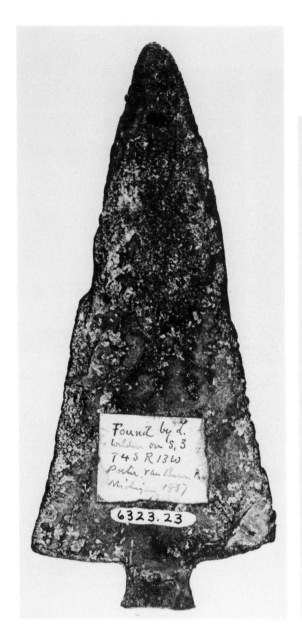

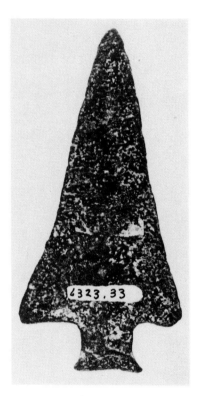

| 218 | 220 | 224 |
| :---: | :---: | :---: |
| Van Buren Co., Mich. | Iosco Co., Mich. | Michigan (County unknown) |

**Reference:** No. 220 is pictured by Perino (1968b).

**Comments:** To the author's knowledge, this form has not been named in Michigan. The material is native copper.

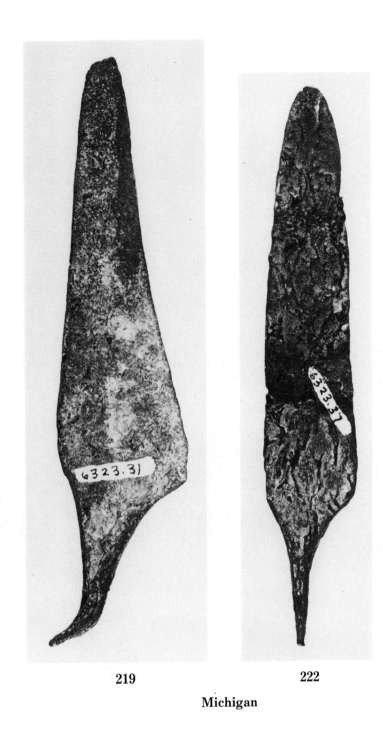

219         222

**Michigan**

**Reference:** No. 219 is pictured by Perino (1968b). See Old Copper Complex.

**Comments:** For information on the Old Copper Complex, see Wormington (1958). The examples shown here are made from native copper.

807
Alpena Co., Mich.

217
Shawano Co., Wisc.

806
Alpena Co., Mich.

623
Kent Co., Mich.

**Reference:** See Old Copper Complex.

**Comments:** These examples are made of native copper from the Wisconsin and upper Great Lakes area.

3

4

5

Group 733
Tishomingo Co., Miss.

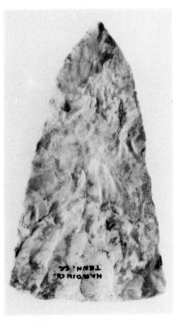
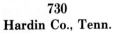

730
Hardin Co., Tenn.

729
Hardin Co., Tenn.

731
Tishomingo Co., Miss.

**Reference:** Shown here are miscellaneous triangular forms typical of the lower Tennessee River Valley. See Morrow Mountain Rounded Base and Jeff points.

**Comments:** Nos. 729, 730, and 731 are planoconvex in cross-section. The base has multiple parallel flake thinning on the flat side. This method of thinning produces a curved basal edge. This thinning, in addition to polishing of the basal edge, indicates that the form was probably used as a projectile point rather than a knife. To the author's knowledge, this form has not been named. Forms similar to Nos. 3 and 4 in Group 733 found in Illinois are called Hopewell points (LaDassor, 1958). No. 5 in Group 733 is the typical Jeff form.

**51**
**Howard Co., Ind.**

**403**
**Lawrence Co., Ind.**

**570**
**Lyon Co., Ky.**

**Reference:** No data.

**Comments:** The total distributional area for this form is not known. It is found sporadically in the states shown above, but it is not found in numbers anywhere. To the author's knowledge, this form has not been named.

455

592
Marshall Co., Ky.

593
Hart Co., Ky.

**Reference:** No data.

**Comments:** Notched stemmed and double corner notched forms are rare, especially the example from Dickson County, Tennessee, shown in Group 594. Blades similar to No. 592 have been called "double notched turkey-tails".

Dickson Co., Tenn.

Trigg Co., Ky.

Group 594

233

**6**
**Lawrence Co., Mo.**

**634**
**McNairy Co., Tenn.**

**661**
**Lyon Co., Ky.**

**635**
**Lyon Co., Ky.**

**662**
**Lyon Co., Ky.**

**Reference:** Polished blades and projectile points.

**Comments:** These types of artifacts are relatively scarce with no particular form predominating. Flaking scars rarely are completely obliterated and often the polishing is more extensive on one side than the other. The Etley (variation) No. 273 in this publication is polished on the reverse side.

**525**
**Tishomingo Co., Miss.**

**Reference:** No data.

**Comments:** This example is coated with a water deposited stain or mineral and the appearance of the material is not unlike hematite. Other examples of blades and projectile points with this coating are known from the southeastern United States and many are found in streams or rivers. The stem on this example is similar to Archaic forms found in the area.

427              20

Limestone Co., Ala.

**Reference:** See Copena and Bakers Creek.

**Comments:** The two forms referred to above are shown here for comparison. The Bakers Creek form No. 20 is sometimes called Stemmed Copena. The Copena (shield form) No. 427 should not be confused with the Mineral Springs and Gahagan knife forms.

**Group 133**

**Reference:** See Cotaco Creek.

**Comments:** These examples are from a cache of 34 pieces and were found in Lauderdale County, Alabama. The two hole gorget is planoconvex in cross-section and is drilled from the flat side, a characteristic of the Adena gorget form (Lewis and Kneberg, 1957b). The Cotaco Creek knife form shown here is rare.

**Group 736**

**Reference:** See Fractured Base Stem points.

**Comments:** The two stemmed base examples shown on the right have fractured bases identical to Nos. 10, 620, and 621 in this book. All of these examples appear to be salvaged parts of points and were used as a material source for flake blades. This method of taking the flakes off in a curve is unique in North America but the method is highly developed in some of the early cultures from Mexico (Perino, 1983). These examples are from the Pickwick Basin area of northeastern Mississippi and apparently are only found in the lower Tennessee River Valley.

# SELECTED REFERENCES

Anderson, Peggy.
1984 "Buffalo River Cache". *The Central States Archaeological Journal*, Vol. 31, No. 1, p. 19.

Baldwin, John, Editor.
1979a *The Redskin*, Vol. 14, No. 2, p. 55.
1979b *The Redskin*, Vol. 14, No. 3, p. 24.
1980 *The Redskin*, Vol. 15, No. 3 and 4, p. 117.

Bell, Robert E.
1958 *Guide to the Identification of Certain American Indian Projectile Points, Special Bulletin No. 1.* Oklahoma Anthropological Society, Norman, OK, 104 p.
1960 *Guide to the Identification of Certain American Indian Projectile Points, Special Bulletin No. 2.* Oklahoma Anthropological Society, Norman, OK, 105 p.

Berner, Jack, Editor.
1970 *The Redskin*, Vol. 1, No. 2, p. 44.

Broyles, Bette J.
1971 Secondary Preliminary Report: The St. Albans Site, Kanawha County, West Virginia. *Report of Archaeological Investigations Number 3.* West Virginia Geological and Economic Survey, Morgantown, WV, 104 p.

Bullen, Ripley P.
1968 *A Guide to the Identification of Florida Projectile Points.* Florida State Museum, University of Florida, Gainesville, FL, 50 p.

Burford, C. C., Editor.
1948 *Journal of the Illinois State Archaeological Society,* Vol. 5, No. 4, p. 6.

Cambron, James W., and David C. Hulse.
1975 *Handbook of Alabama Archaeological, Part I, Point Types.* Archaeological Research Association of Alabama, Inc., 134 p.

Chapman, Carl H., and Eleanor F. Chapman.
1972 *Indians and Archaeology of Missouri, Missouri Handbook Number Five.* University of Missouri Press, Columbia, MO, 161 p.

Cloud, Ron.
1969 "Cache River Sidenotched Points". *Central States Archaeological Journal*, Vol. 16, No. 3, pp. 118-119.

Converse, Robert N.
1973 *Ohio Flint Types.* The Archaeological Society of Ohio, Columbus, OH, 76 p.

Cooper, Peter P.
1970 "Rowan Points". *Central States Archaeological Journal*, Vol. 17, No. 3, pp. 113-115.

DeCamp, Darwin K.
1967 "The Clipped Wing Point". *Central States Archaeological Journal*, Vol. 14, No. 3, pp. 108-112.

Duncan, James, Editor.
1972 *Central States Archaeological Journal*, Vol. 19, No. 2, p. 69.
1973a *Central States Archaeological Journal*, Vol. 20, No. 3, p. 129.
1973b *Central States Archaeological Journal*, Vol. 20, No. 4, pp. 145-191.

Edler, Robert.
1970 "The Heavy Duty Point". *The Redskin*, Vol. 5, No. 2, pp. 16-17.
1975 Personal correspondence.

Ferguson, J. C.
1963 "A Mistaken Land Owner". *Central States Archaeological Journal*, Vol. 10, No. 2, pp. 53-54.

Fowler, Melvin L., Editor.
1951 *Illinois State Archaeological Society, New Series*, Vol. 2, No. 1, pp. 16-28.

Fundaburk, Emma Lila, and Mary Douglas Foreman.
1957 *Sun Circles and Human Hands, The Southeast Indians - Art and Industry.* Paragon Press, Montgomery, AL, 232 p.

Grimm, E. R.
1953 *Prehistoric Art, A Picture Study of Ancient America Thru Tools and Artifacts.* The Greater St. Louis Archaeological Society, Wellington Print, St. Louis, MO, 160 p.

Guthe, Alfred K.
1963 *The Tennessee Archaeologist*, Vol. 19, No. 2, p. 68.

Holmes, W. H.
1919 *Handbook of Aboriginal American Antiquities, Part I Introductory the Lithic Industries, Bulletin 60.* Smithsonian Institution, Government Printing Office, Washington, D.C., 380 p.

Kizzia, Glen L.
1968 "Burial Customs of the Caddo". *Central States Archaeological Journal*, Vol. 15, No. 2, pp. 59-63.

Kneberg, Madeline.
1956 "Some Important Projectile Point Types Found in the Tennessee Area". *The Tennessee Archaeologist*, Vol. 12, No. 1, pp. 17-28.
1957 "Chipped Stone Artifacts of the Tennessee River Valley Area". *The Tennessee Archaeologist*, Vol. 13, No. 1, pp. 55-56.74

Knoblock, Byron W.
1939 *Bannerstones of the North American Indian.* Publication of Byron W. Knoblock, LaGrange, IL, 596 p.

Knoblock, Byron W., Editor.
1948 *Illinois State Archaeological Society Journal*, Vol. 5, No. 4, p. 13.
1955 *Central States Archaeological Journal*, Vol. 2, No. 2, p. 64.

Kramer, Leon.
1947 "Prehistoric Ohio Flint, Primitive Material Sources - Projectile Forms and a Tribute to Their Art Phases". *Illinois State Archaeological Society Journal*, Vol. 5, No. 2, pp. 32-51.

LaDassor, Gray R., Editor.
1958a *Central States Archaeological Journal*, Vol. 4, No. 4, pp. 134-135.
1958b *Central States Archaeological Journal*, Vol. 5, No. 2, p. 46.
1958c *Central States Archaeological Journal*, Vol. 5, No. 2, p. 73.
1966a *Central States Archaeological Journal*, Vol. 13, No. 2, pp. 52-55.
1966b *The Redskin*, Vol. 2, No. 2l, pp. 10-12.
1974 *The Redskin*, Vol. 9, No. 4, p. 140.
1976 *The Redskin*, Vol. 11, No. 1, p. 17.
1977 *The Redskin*, Vol. 12, No. 1, p. 21.

Lewis, T. M. N., and Madeline Kneberg Lewis.
1961 *Eva: An Archaic Site, A University of Tennessee Study in Anthropology.* University of Tennessee Press, Knoxville, TN, 174 p.

Lewis, T. M. N., and Madeline Kneberg, Editors.
1951 "Early Projectile Point Forms, and Examples from Tennessee". *The Tennessee Archaeologist*, Vol. 7, No. 1, pp. 6-9.
1953 *The Tennessee Archaeologist*, Vol. 11, No. 2, pp. 83-84.
1957a "The Camp Creek Site". *The Tennessee Archaeologist*, Vol. 13, No. 1, pp. 1-48.
1957b "The Old Sarge Says". *The Tennessee Archaeologist*, Vol. 13, No. 1, pp. 67-72.
1962 "The Old Sarge Says". *The Tennessee Archaeologist*, Vol. 18, No. 2, pp. 91-99.

Logan, Wilfred D.
1952 *Graham Cave, an Archaic Site in Montgomery County, Missouri, With an Appendix: Recent Excavations in Graham Cave by Carl H. Chapman, Memoir No. 2, May, 1952.* Missouri Archaeological Society, Columbia, MO, 101 p.

Macgowan, Kenneth, and Joseph A. Hester, Jr.
1962 Early Man in the New World. *The Natural History Library*, Anchor Books, Doubleday and Company, Inc., Garden City, NY, 333 p.

McGahey, Samuel O.
1981 "The Coldwater and Related Late Paleo Indian Projectile Points". *Mississippi Archaeology*, Vol. 16, No. 2, pp. 39-51.
1985 Personal communication.

McPherson, H. R., Editor.
1963 *Central States Archaeological Journal*, Vol. 10, No. 2, p. 57.

Moorehead, W. K.
1910    *The Stone Age in North America, Volume I*, Boston, MA.

Patterson, J. T.
1936    The Corner-Tang Flint Artifacts of Texas, *The University of Texas Bulletin* No. 3618, May 8, 1936. The University of Texas, Austin, TX, 54 p.

Perino, Gregory.
1947    "Cahokia Notes". *Illinois State Archaeological Society Journal*, Vol. 5, No. 2, p. 57.

1962    "Prehistoric Knives in the Middle Mississippi Valley". *Central States Archaeological Journal*, Vol. 9, No. 2, pp. 46-53.

1963    "Tentative Classification of Two Projectile Points and One Knife from West-Central Illinois". *Central States Archaeological Journal*, Vol. 10, No. 3, pp. 95-100.

1967a    *The Cherry Valley Mounds and Banks Mound 3, Memoir No. 1.* Central States Archaeological Societies, Inc., St. Louis, MO, 88 p.

1967b    "Some Acquisitions by the Gilcrease Institute in 1966". *Central States Archaeological Journal*, Vol. 14, No. 2, p. 68.

1968a    *Guide to the Identification of Certain American Indian Projectile Points, Special Bulletin No. 3.* Oklahoma Anthropological Society, Norman, OK, 104 p.

1968b    "The Shiney 'Red Stone' That Wouldn't Break". *Central States Archaeological Journal*, Vol. 15, No. 3, pp. 101-102.

1969a    "The Morse Archaic Knife". *Central States Archaeological Journal*, Vol. 16, No. 2, pp. 86-87.

1969b    "North Points or Blades". *Central States Archaeological Journal*, Vol. 16, No. 4, pp. 184-187.

1970a    "Some Outstanding Artifacts Acquired by the Gilcrease Institute in 1969". *Central States Archaeological Journal*, Vol. 17, No. 1, pp. 31-35.

1970b    "The Stilwell II Site, Pike County, Illinois". *Central States Archaeological Journal*, Vol. 17, No. 3, pp. 119-121.

1971a    *Guide to the Identification of Certain American Indian Projectile Points, Special Bulletin No. 4.* Oklahoma Anthropological Society, Norman, OK, 105 p.

1971b    Mississippian Site Archaeology in Illinois: I. Illinois Archaeological Survey, Inc., *Bulletin No. 8*, Urbana, IL.

1972    "A Little About Ovoid and Tanged Knives". *Central States Archaeological Journal*, Vol. 19, No. 3, pp. 100-105.

1976a    "Lightening Does Strike Twice or Five Aces Beats a Full House". *Central States Archaeological Journal*, Vol. 23, No. 3, pp. 116-119.

1976b    "Some Texas Knives". *Central States Archaeological Journal*, Vol. 23, No. 4, pp. 158-162.

1976c    "A New Point Type". *Central States Archaeological Journal*, Vol. 23-24, No. 2, p. 62.

1977    "The Mahaffey Point". *Central States Archaeological Journal*, Vol. 24, No. 4, pp. 164-166.

1982    Personal correspondence.

1983    Personal communication.

1984    Personal correspondence.

1985a    Personal correspondence.

1985b    *Selected Preforms, Points and Knives of the North American Indians*, Vol. 1. Publication of Gregory Perino, Idabel, OK, 404 p.

Puckett, Doug.
1983    *Field Guide to Point Types of the Tennessee River Basin Region.* Publication of Doug Puckett, Sheffield, AL, 30 p.

Roberts, Jack C.
1968    "The Great Stone Faces". *The Redskin*, Vol. 3, No. 2, pp. 60-61.

Roshto, James.
1983    "The Bascom Blades". *Central States Archaeological Journal*, Vol. 30, No. 1, p. 28.

Russell, Virgil Y.
1959    "The Yuma-A Symphony in Stone". *Central States Archaeological Journal*, Vol. 6, No. 2, pp. 51-54.

Scott, Jerry.
1974    "A Copena Point Cache". *Central States Archaeological Journal*, Vol. 21, No. 3, p. 143.

Seeman, Mark F.
1975    "Buck Creek Barbed Projectile Points". *Central States Archaeological Journal*, Vol. 22, No. 3, pp. 106-108.

Thompson, Ben W.
1984    *Who's Who in Indian Relics, No. 6.* Publication of Ben Thompson, Kirkwood, MO, 344 p.

Thompson, Ben W., Editor.
1968    *Central States Archaeological Journal*, Vol. 15, No. 3, pp. 95-120.

1969    *Central States Archaeological Journal*, Vol. 16, No. 1, p. 24.

1970    *Central States Archaeological Journal*, Vol. 17, No. 3, p. 136.

1971a    *Central States Archaeological Journal*, Vol. 18, No. 1, p. 40.

1971b    *Central States Archaeological Journal*, Vol. 18, No. 1, p. 60.

Titterington, P. F.
1938    *The Cahokia Mound Group and Its Village Site Materials.* St. Louis, MO, 40 p.

1950    "Some Non-Pottery Sites in St. Louis Area". *Illinois State Archaeological Society Journal*, Vol. 1, No. 1, pp. 19-30.

Townsend, Earl C., Jr.
1959    *Birdstones of the North American Indian.* Publication of Earl C. Townsend, Jr., Indianapolis, IN, 719 p.

Van Blair, Dale, Editor.
1981    *Central States Archaeological Journal*, Vol. 28, No. 3, p. 138.

1982a    *Central States Archaeological Journal*, Vol. 29, No. 1, p. 53.

1982b    *Central States Archaeological Journal*, Vol. 29, No. 2, p. 107.

1982c    *Central States Archaeological Journal*, Vol. 29, No. 4, p. 207.

1983a    *Central States Archaeological Journal*, Vol. 30, No. 3, pp. 144-146.

1983b    *Central States Archaeological Journal*, Vol. 30, No. 3, p. 160.

Wadlow, W. L.
1951    *The Snyders Site, Calhoun County, Illinois.* The Greater St. Louis Archaeological Society, St. Louis, MO.

Webb, William S., and David L. DeJarnette.
1942    *An Archaeological Survey of the Pickwick Basin in the Adjacent Portions of the States of Alabama, Mississippi, and Tennessee, Bureau of American Ethnology, Bulletin 129.* Smithsonian Institution, Government Printing Office, Washington, D.C., 536 p.

Webb, William S., and William D. Funkhouser.
1928    Ancient Life in Kentucky. *The Kentucky Geological Survey*, Series Six, Volume Thirty-Four, Frankfort, KY, 349 p.

Wilson, Thomas.
1897    "Arrowheads, Spearheads, and Knives of Prehistoric Times", *Annual Report of the Board of Regents of the Smithsonian Institution, Report of the U. S. National Museum Part I.* Government Printing Office, Washington, D. C., pp. 823-988.

Wilkes, Jeff.
1982    "The Resharpening of Flint Blades". *Central States Archaeological Journal*, Vol. 29, No. 3, p. 146.

Wormington, H. M.
1958    *Ancient Man in North America*, Popular Series No. 4. Denver Museum of Natural History, Denver, Colorado, 322 p.

Young, Bennett H.
1910    The Prehistoric Men of Kentucky, *Filson Club Publications* Number Twenty-Five. Filson Club, Louisville, Kentucky, 343 p.